**Discovering Shakespeare**

# Romeo and Juliet

## A WORKBOOK FOR STUDENTS

## YOUNG ACTORS SERIES

If you require pre-publication information about upcoming Smith and Kraus books, you may receive our semi-annual catalogue, free of charge, by sending your name and address to *Smith and Kraus Catalogue*, P.O. Box 127, One Main Street, Lyme, NH 03768. Or call us at (800) 895-4331, fax (603) 795-4427.

Discovering Shakespeare

# Romeo and Juliet
## A WORKBOOK FOR STUDENTS

Written and Edited by Fredi Olster
and Rick Hamilton

*Young Actors Series*

SK

A Smith and Kraus Book

A Smith and Kraus Book
Published by Smith and Kraus, Inc.
One Main Street, PO Box 127, Lyme, NH 03768

Copyright © 1996 by F. Olster and R. Hamilton
All rights reserved
Manufactured in the United States of America
Cover and Text Design by Julia Hill
Cover Art by Irene Kelly

First Edition: June 1996
10 9 8 7 6 5 4 3 2

Library of Congress Cataloging-in-Publication Date

Discovering Shakespeare : Romeo and Juliet : a workbook for students / edited by Fredi Olster and Rick Hamilton.
--1st ed.  p.  cm.  -- (Young actors series)
Includes an abridgement of the original text, an adaptation into vernacular English,
and discussions of Shakespearean English, character analysis, and performance and production.
Includes bibliographical references  (p.  ).
ISBN 1-57525-045-4 (pbk.)
1. Shakespeare, William, 1564-1616.  Romeo and Juliet--Problems, exercises, etc.
2. Shakespeare, william, 1564-1616--Outlines, syllabi, etc.
3. Shakespeare, William, 1564-1616--Dramatic production.
4. Shakespeare, William, 1564-1616--Adaptation.
I. Olster, Fredi.  II. Hamilton, Rick.  III. Series: Young actor series.
PR2831.D57    1996
822.3'3--dc20    96-15959
CIP

# Contents

# "How came these things to pass?"

HOW THESE BOOKS CAME
TO BE WRITTEN

I have spent most of my life working as a Shakespearean actress. Yet, when I was growing up and studying Shakespeare in school, I hated it! I came to realize that many of my teachers also hated it. And who can blame any of us, we didn't understand it for the most part.

It wasn't until I started acting in Shakespeare's plays at the Oregon Shakespeare Festival in 1970 that I began to feel differently. There, I met Angus Bowmer, the founder of the festival and director of the first play I was to do there, *The Merchant of Venice,* and Rick Hamilton, a young actor at the festival, who was later to become my husband.

Between them, they taught me to love the language and to appreciate the timelessness of the stories. And now, of course, I'm hooked. I would rather act in a play by Shakespeare than any other playwright.

I've come to realize that my experience with Shakespeare is not unique. And it was my desire to share what I have learned from Angus and Rick and the many other directors and actors I've worked with over the years that inspired me to write this workbook.

The immediate impetus came though while I was doing a production of *Christmas Carol* in San Francisco. I was playing Mrs. Fezziwig who is a delightful character but who isn't in a lot of scenes. So I had a great deal of time for other activities.

One of them was to start work on *All's Well That Ends Well,* which I was to be in when *Christmas Carol* closed. "All's Well" was a play that I was totally unfamiliar with. I was sitting in my dressing room with my Shakespeare glossaries, dictionaries and various copies of the play doing my *homework* when my friend Sarah came in and asked what I was up to.

Sarah was then twelve and was playing Young Belle in our production. She and I were old friends having worked together on two shows in the past. I told Sarah what I was doing and she asked if she could read "All's Well" with me. I said "sure" and we proceeded to read the Helena/Parolles scene in Act 1 together.

Note that this is a particularly difficult scene, full of double entendre, sexual innuendo and very complex language. We read together and looked up all the words we didn't grasp.

Let me say that I have to do this whenever I work on a Shakespeare play that I don't know well. The words he used are different from the ones we now use. In the four hundred years since he wrote these plays, the English language has changed and some of the words Shakespeare used have gone out of fashion or have evolved in their meanings so that we no longer easily understand them.

But with a little practice and *homework* we quickly realize that the ideas he wrote about remain extremely applicable to us.

I came to understand this even more clearly when, after Sarah and I had finished the scene and had discussed what it meant, Sarah said to me, "I'm going to read this to my friends tomorrow at school, this stuff is great and it's so sexy." Well at that moment I realized once again the absolute brilliance of Shakespeare. He had the power to reach out through those four hundred years that separated him and Sarah and thoroughly excite her interest.

Sarah is now a young lady of fourteen and not only has she continued to be excited by Shakespeare, but she has passed on her interest to her younger sister Julia who is ten.

The question then became, how can we (by this time Rick agreed to work on this project with me) make Shakespeare accessible to kids who don't have an actor to sit down and read it with? And that's how the idea for this format came about.

Our objective became: tell the story, introduce the characters, and let Shakespeare's ideas come ringing through. The difficulty, of course, is that wonderfully complex language of Shakespeare's. So we decided the best way to introduce Shakespeare to people who were not familiar with him was, as I had done with Sarah, to translate him into the *vernacular*–that is, our equivalent everyday language.

That way, the new student of Shakespeare can begin to understand the story, the characters and the ideas without the added obstacle of the four-hundred-year-old words.

Once these elements become clearer and the reader starts to discover the beauty of Shakespeare, as Sarah did, it then becomes even more thrilling to go back to the original language which is, needless to say, so much richer and more poetic than anything we have replaced it with.

Let us point out here that this workbook is only meant as an introduction to Shakespeare. We are actors and not scholars and would not pretend competency in that world.

Our main objective is to instill a love of Shakespeare and to encourage the next generation of young people to attend our theatres with a true desire to see and support and perhaps act in the works of the incomparable master.

It is our sincere hope that the users of these workbooks will discover the joys of Shakespeare sooner than we were able to and will be tempted to move on to Shakespeare's complete versions of the plays with enthusiasm and with ease.

# How to Use this Book

The Discovering Shakespeare edition of *Romeo and Juliet*, with its abridged version of the play along with the vernacular translation and supportive chapters, is designed for multiple uses.

1). It serves as a workbook to help in the study of Shakespeare's language. By reading scenes aloud, and using the accompanying vernacular translation to facilitate comprehension, the student will find it easier to understand the language and plot of the play thereby making the study of Shakespeare an enjoyable experience.

2). It serves as a launching pad for a *reading* of the play. Students take on the individual parts, doing research into the characters and then, with scripts in hand, read the play aloud.

3). It serves as an aid in organizing a simple production of the play for classroom performance.

It is up to the facilities available and the interest of the various class situations to determine what would be most useful for them.

We have included information about *performance* because this material is vital for the understanding of Shakespeare. Shakespeare was first and foremost a man of the theatre. To understand him, it is necessary to understand the medium he was writing for.

It is our intention that the vernacular version be employed to facilitate understanding of Shakespeare's language, and that Shakespeare's own words be used for performance.

Also, please note that the suggested stage directions, acting notes, character interpretations, etc. reflect our personal opinions and should merely be thought of as a starting place—none of this is in stone—Shakespeare is open to interpretation. Be free and creative in your choices and your work. You are the next generation of Shakespeare students, interpreters, audience and performers—he is now in your hands—serve him well.

*"\*" within the play indicates suggestion to see chapter on acting techniques and theatrical conventions*

# "Here's much to do with hate, but more with love."

A LOOK AT SOME OF THE IDEAS IN *ROMEO AND JULIET*

"All my fortunes at thy foot I'll lay and follow thee my lord throughout the world."

These words lie at the heart of *Romeo and Juliet*. This is a love story about two young people whose purity of passion lends them great stature. How many people do you know, who would not only express that kind of love and commitment, but be willing to back it up with their lives? Romeo and Juliet do just that in the course of this play. Their love is so complete, so true and yet ultimately, so impossible!

Shakespeare is not talking about a teenage crush. He is talking about a love that will not be denied. He is also talking about a society whose rules and customs do deny it.

In *A Midsummer Night's Dream*, a play written at about the same time, one of Shakespeare's characters says "the course of true love never did run smooth." In *Romeo and Juliet*, Shakespeare demonstrates just how true that statement can be.

Let's take a look at the society in which Romeo and Juliet lived, and the rules and customs that guided it, to see what these obstacles to true love's course were.

The major obstacle, is the feud which exists between their families. Shakespeare tells us very little about the feud except to say that it is an "ancient quarrel." The "brawl" that opens the play is one of three recent eruptions between the Capulets and the Montagues.

In Shakespeare's time, feuds were fairly common largely due to the obsession with honor which was so prevalent at the time. The accrual and preservation of honor was the driving force behind life for noble renaissance men.

Renaissance is defined by the dictionary as rebirth. What was being reborn was a way of life and thought based on ancient Greece and Rome. One particular idea from the ancient world, which has a direct bearing on this play is the concept of *honor*.

According to the Greek philosopher, Aristotle, honor was the reward for living a virtuous life. A virtuous life consisted of serving mankind by being just, valorous, moderate in thought and action, showing a lofty and courageous spirit, being wise, magnanimous and on and on. Sort of like superman!

It was supposed that living a virtuous life was the way to go, and that virtue would have its rewards: namely receiving honors. A wonderful ideal, but the reality was quite another story.

Over time, the desire for honor came to overshadow the striving for virtue, and for the renaissance nobleman, the winning and maintaining of honor became his prime objective.

Honor was a delicate thing though, and could easily be lost through slights or insults. The man of honor had to be constantly on guard to defend his status, which he would do by challenging an offending party to a duel. If victorious, this not only preserved his honor, but won him more by proving his valor and bravery.

These people who were adhering to this code of honor were not members of a gang living in a ghetto, but incredibly wealthy and powerful men who were the so-called pillars of society and who were running the governments.

An example of the ridiculous extremes to which this ideal could be taken is seen here: Elizabeth the First (who was queen while Shakespeare was writing) gave one of her courtiers a chess piece made of gold. Another of her favorites felt that he should have received a gift of equal value and, since he hadn't, his honor had been offended. So deeply wounded was he, that he publicly insulted the man who'd been given the chess piece, who in turn, challenged him to a duel!

All sorts of rules and regulations were devised regarding honor, and these were formally written up and became known as the *renaissance code of honor.*

This code was catalogued into all sorts of categories, subcatagories, types, classifications, subclassifications, and so on an on ad infinitum.

For instance, there were rules about:

• who could be worthy of honor and thereby participate in the big honor challenge (for the most part, the nobility had the lock on honor—although soldiers and gentlemen could work their way in, to some degree, under certain circumstances)

• who you could insult and who was out of range (you should only insult your equals and it was best to do it face to face)

Then there were rules about the various *forms* of the insult:

• there was the contemptuous insult which reduced one's dignity by belittling it

• there was the spiteful insult which was messing with someone just for the heck of it and which didn't benefit the one who offered the insult

• there was the insult of insolence which consisted of mistreating everyone in general so as to prove your superiority.

As you can see, some pretty fine hairs were being split to determine these distinctions!

Then there was the question of what motivated your insult:

• was it motivated by ignorance? (for example, in England and France, it was an insult for a stranger not to kiss the ladies of the household when introduced to them, while in Spain and Italy, it was an insult if you did! So, if a Frenchman kissed an Italian's wife, he could be forgiven, but if a Spaniard kissed that same Italian wife, he could be skewered!)

• was duress the motivating factor? (You're in a crowd and someone pushes into you, which causes you to push into someone else—even though you have pushed into him, you are not insulting him, because you were pushed and therefore under duress—but what about the guy who pushed you?)

• was this an insult of passion, motivated by love of a woman or to defend a benefactor, relative or friend?

Then there was the insult of insults, the deliberate insult—this is your premeditated insult, with malice aforethought, intended to cause injury!

Then there was the debate over the method of conveyance of insult—which was worse:

• the action insult (a physical insult, affecting the body)

• the verbal insult (a spoken insult, affecting the soul). Take your pick!

Further categories of insult were:

• the general insult ("you are a scoundrel!")

• the specific insult ("you are a scoundrel because you kicked my horse!")

Then, of course, there were the various ways in which one could respond to an insult:

• if slight enough, it could be ignored—but rarely was

•or you could call the guy a liar and get on with the fight—which is what most everybody wanted anyway because whoever won would get more honor!

In such a society, it's not hard to see how a feud between two noble families could erupt and thrive!

This obsession with honor is evident throughout *Romeo and Juliet* and it is the mechanism which drives so many promising young people to their deaths.

The first scene of the play illustrates many of the rules of honor. Here, we see the servants of the feuding households almost parodying the honor code of their masters. Servants, remember, were not capable of honor because they were not nobly born. They could exhibit noble traits—namely honesty and loyalty—but anything approaching the heroic, was out of the question.

Ironically, Shakespeare has four young servants, incapable of achieving honor themselves, about to start a fight about honor! They are like children trying to play a grown-up game, not really sure of the rules, but doing their level best to pretend they know them.

SAMPSON:
I strike quickly, being moved.
GREGORY:
But thou art not quickly moved to strike.
SAMPSON:
A dog of the house of Montague moves me.
GREGORY:
Draw; here comes two of the house of Montague.
SAMPSON:
My naked weapon is out; quarrel, I will back thee.
GREGORY:
How? Turn thy back and run?
SAMPSON:
Fear me not. Let us have the law on our side; let them begin.
GREGORY:
I will frown as I pass by, and let them take it as they list.
SAMPSON:
Nay. I will bite my thumb at them, which is disgrace to them if they bear it.
[enter Abram and Balthasar]
ABRAM:
Do you bite your thumb at us, sir?
SAMPSON:
I do bite my thumb, sir.
ABRAM:
Do you bite your thumb at us, sir?
SAMPSON: [aside to Gregory]
Is the law on our side, if I say—ay?
GREGORY:
No.
SAMPSON: [turning back to Abram]
No, sir, I do not bite my thumb at you, sir;

but I bite my thumb, sir.
GREGORY: [to Abram]
Do you quarrel, sir?
ABRAM:
Quarrel, sir? No, sir.
SAMPSON:
But if you do, sir, I am for you; I serve as good a man as you.
ABRAM:
No better.
SAMPSON:
Well, sir.
GREGORY: [aside to Sampson]
Say—better; here comes one of my master's kinsmen.
SAMPSON:
Yes, better, sir.
ABRAM:
You lie.
SAMPSON:
Draw, if you be men.

Let's take a look at how this scene progresses from comic bragging to mayhem. The scene opens with two Capulet servants, Sampson and Gregory. Sampson is telling Gregory, in effect, how brave he is. (This is his first mistake—while honor and glory is what all men are trying to achieve—bragging about your prowess is bad form—you may just have to back it up!)

After Gregory makes several jokes at Sampson's expense, two Montague servants appear, Abram and Balthasar. The first thing Sampson does is *bite his thumb* at them which is the Elizabethan equivalent of *flipping them off*. Abram takes the bait and asks Sampson if he is biting his thumb at him. If Sampson were to say 'yes', this would be admitting that he was trying to pick a fight, and therefore would be at fault—his objective is to get the Montague boys to start the fight so that he can appear blameless. Sampson therefore answers, noncommittally, "I do bite my thumb, sir." (Notice all the *sirs* in this passage—very honorable!)

Abram repeats his question, further daring Sampson to respond. (Note that Abram also wants a fight—but they are all involved in that fine point of honor—getting the other guy to be at fault by starting it!) Sampson and Gregory huddle for a moment and decide they have to say "no" but Sampson points out once again that a thumb is definitely being bitten.

Here we have Sampson at his ridiculous best—walking around with his thumb in his teeth, hoping Abram will take offense and start a fight—yet denying he's trying to provoke him. This is exactly what many of the noblemen of the time were doing to each other.

Gregory now chimes in and asks Abram if he is

trying to pick a quarrel. Abram must say "no" because otherwise, he would be at fault!

Sampson now takes it a step further and says, in effect, you'd better not be because I can take you and adds the taunt "I serve as good a man as you." Abram replies threateningly, "No better" because if either were to say my boss is better than your boss, that would be an insult and would start a fight.

All Sampson can think to say is, "well, sir" (pretty tame for all that bragging he had done earlier!) Since neither side is willing to step over the line, the confrontation could very well have ended here, except that Gregory sees Tybalt coming. He knows Tybalt is always looking for trouble and is confident that he will back them up once the fighting begins, so he tells Sampson to say "better" which Sampson does. Abram is then obliged to call Sampson a liar. If you were called a liar, you had to fight to defend your honor, and so the brawl begins.

Up to now nothing has really been at stake because the participants have all been servants, but with the arrival of Benvolio and Tybalt, things get serious. They are both members of the noble class, so what they do counts!

Their fight, (which Tybalt instigates) leads to Capulet and Montague coming on and threatening each other. The resulting brawl raises the tension between the families and sets the stage for the rest of the play.

All this trouble has been caused by an "airy word" as the Prince points out. Here we see the power of language in action!

Later in the scene we meet Romeo and we see that he is not concerned with all this honor business. He is in love and his focus is elsewhere. In spite of his lack of concern, honor nevertheless, will be his downfall as we shall see.

In Act 1 scene 2, we encounter another aspect of honor; the extreme formality which it required. One had to be very careful about one's choice of words in order to avoid the consequences of the "airy word." Conversations often became overly formal and stilted. We see this with Paris and Capulet. Paris is a count, Capulet a lord, and each is trying to be more formal and more polite and thereby–according to theory– more honorable.

The Capulet party is another scene that deals with aspects of the honor code. The scene begins with the three lads deciding to crash a party–this was not an unheard of custom at the time, and Mercutio's having been invited is in their favor–but circumstances being as they are, it was a rather bold move to enter the house of your avowed enemy.

They enter and come face to face with Lord Capulet. This is an important moment. Capulet knows who they are (in spite of their masks) and is well within his rights to refuse them entrance. He chooses to let them in. He does this because he truly wants the feud to cease and besides the Prince has just told him, in no uncertain terms, that it had better end or else! The point is, he chooses not to be insulted– besides this is a party! He asks them in, tells them to dance and have a great time. Unfortunately the same cannot be said of Tybalt.

Tybalt recognizes Romeo's voice and this is all Tybalt needs to get beside himself with rage. He immediately assumes Romeo's presence at the party to be an affront to his honor and he tells his uncle about it assuming he too will be outraged. Capulet not only dismisses Tybalt's report of Romeo's presence, but he nails Tybalt calling him a "saucy boy" and praises Romeo's good reputation in Verona. Tybalt is furious and wants revenge! The next morning, Tybalt sends a formal challenge to Romeo's house.

In Act 3 scene 1, all this business about honor comes to a head. Tybalt is out looking for Romeo when he comes across Benvolio and Mercutio. Mercutio proceeds to taunt Tybalt in much the same manner as the servants went at each other in Act 1 scene 1.

Mercutio despises Tybalt for his priggish behavior and his obsession with honor and is itching to cut him down.

Romeo comes into this scene as happy as he can be, he has just married Juliet and is anticipating nightfall when he can climb the rope ladder and be with her. Tybalt delivers a direct challenge to Romeo and Romeo, not wanting to fight with his new cousin, declines the challenge. Mercutio, as Romeo's best friend, and avowed despiser of Tybalt, takes up the challenge and the fight is on. When Romeo tries to break it up, Mercutio is mortally wounded by Tybalt.

Romeo now feels obliged by the code of honor to avenge Mercutio's death by killing Tybalt and in so doing seals his and Juliet's doom. Events have now gone too far; reconciliation of the families is impossible and he knows it. Honor has cost him his chance of happiness.

In a later play, *Henry 4* Part 1, Shakespeare has the character Fallstaff come right out and flatly state that honor is just not worth it. In *Romeo and Juliet* he lets the characters' actions speak for him, but his message is the same.

Another aspect of life that creates obstacles for Romeo and Juliet, is the way in which marriages were arranged. Among the nobility, marriage frequently had more to do with money and property than with love.

Fathers had complete control over who their daughters would marry. The wishes of the daughter might be considered, but in the end money and power usually ruled. So it is with Juliet. Her father is looking for a suitable match–Montagues are out of the question–but a kinsman of the Prince–ah!!! Now, there's a chance to kill two birds with one stone. Marrying into the Prince's family would not only bring more honor, but it might align the Prince on the Capulet side of the feud.

At first Capulet wants to wait awhile thinking Juliet is too young to marry, but when Tybalt dies, leaving Capulet without a male heir, something must be done. At this point all considerations of Juliet's wishes vanish–Juliet has now become a bargaining chip.

As Juliet's options diminish, with this decision of her father's, her search for solutions becomes more desperate. From her point of view, she can give up her life, or her reason for living–Romeo. Frantically, she tries to find some way out or around or through, the "stratagems" heaven seems to be practicing on her, but when she awakens in the tomb and finds Romeo dead, she knows there is only one course of action–she takes it without a moment's hesitation.

It was the pressure from her father and from society at large that pushed Juliet into this untenable situation and caused her death.

# "Two households, both alike in dignity"

BRIEF DESCRIPTIONS OF THE CHARACTERS IN *ROMEO AND JULIET*

Imagine a small Italian town surrounded by vineyards and olive trees covering the gently rolling hills which extend in all directions from it. Everything is lush and green and very fertile. The town itself is nestled at the foot of the hills. It begins as a smattering of small cottages at the outskirts, growing more dense as it moves inward and rising to more impressive structures as we reach closer to the center of the town where we find an immense town square.

The wealthiest families have their homes facing the town square, along with the Prince's palace and the town's church.

The square is large, and when the hot summer sun has set and the evening breezes have cooled the stone walkways, the townspeople gather here. They stroll hand in hand and talk about their day. It is here where the old men meet and tell stories of the past, where the neighbor ladies gossip, the servants play betting games and drink wine, and where the young boys and girls strut about pretending to ignore each other and yet furiously flirting with the opposite sex.

This is hot-blooded Italy at the very height of summer. It is here, probably in the late 1300s, in a town called Verona that *Romeo and Juliet* takes place.

|  | Prince |  |
|---|---|---|
| Capulet |  | Montague |
| Lady Capulet |  | Lady Montague |
| Juliet — Paris | Mercutio — Romeo |  |
| Tybalt |  | Benvolio |

The characters in *Romeo and Juliet* come from the three wealthiest and most important families in Verona: the Capulets, the Montagues, and the royal family.

The Prince is head of the royal family and is the ruler of Verona. Two of his kinsmen, Paris and Mercutio, also play important parts in our story–one aligned with the Capulets and the other with the Montagues.

The Capulet family is made up of Lord Capulet, his wife, Lady Capulet, their daughter, Juliet, and Tybalt, nephew to Lady Capulet.

The Montagues are composed of Lord Montague, Lady Montague, their son Romeo, and Romeo's cousin, Benvolio.

Let's take a look at all the characters who appear in *Romeo and Juliet.*

**SERVANTS:**

The first characters we meet are the servants of the two feuding households. Servants at this time were considered part of the household–they were on the Capulet or Montague *team* so to speak–and were totally loyal to their families. They would work for their family for life as their parents no doubt did before them and as their children will no doubt do after them.

They lived with the family and felt the pride and the sorrows of the family as their own. If the family was well off–as were the Capulets and the Montagues–the servants would be well-fed and well-treated, but not well-educated. Education was a luxury for the wealthy and it would be safe to assume that none of these servants could read or write.

**SAMPSON:**

Sampson is a Capulet servant. He is probably in his late teens or early twenties and unmarried. When we meet him, we note his pugnacious nature. He is looking for a fight, itching to stir up some action with the Montagues. Yet, we see what a blowhard Sampson really is when the moment the Montagues appear, he thrusts Gregory forward to begin the action.

**GREGORY:**

Gregory is the brighter of the Capulet servants. He takes what Sampson says and is able to manipulate the language in such a way as to create puns and turns of phrase which keep Sampson on his toes. Gregory too is perfectly willing to fight with the Montagues; note that it is Gregory who, upon seeing Tybalt approach, pushes the fight to its next level.

**ABRAM:**

Abram is most certainly the Montague counterpart of Sampson.

**BALTHASAR:**

Balthasar is Romeo's man—his personal servant. We note that he does not utter a word during the first scene and would probably prefer not to be there. He, like his master, is not obsessed with the feud.

It is later in the play when he goes to Romeo with the news of Juliet's death that we note his compassion and honest concern for his master. This extreme loyalty between servant and master was not uncommon at this time.

**BENVOLIO:**

The name Benvolio means good will, benevolent, kind. These words describe this young member of the Montagues aptly. The first time we encounter Benvolio, he is trying to stop a fight between the Capulet and Montague servants.

He is a peace-loving young man, capable of fighting when pushed (as we see when Tybalt instigates a fight with him) yet he is no *fool for honor* as is Tybalt.

He is honest and reliable. Both the Prince and Montague ask for and trust his judgment on various occasions.

We also see that he is a good friend to both his cousin Romeo and to Mercutio, and while nowhere near as quick-witted or skilled with language as they are, he is no fool. He is the sensible, level-headed member of that trio, the one that can always be counted on in a pinch. It is Benvolio in whom Romeo finally confides his love for Rosaline.

Benvolio is a mature young man with an understanding of other's feelings. It is Benvolio who talks Mercutio out of harassing Romeo after the Capulet party. He had shown similar compassion earlier that morning when he'd spotted Romeo in the woods. Always sensible, Benvolio understands Mercutio's quarrelsome nature and, in a very apt fore-shadowing of things to come, tries to warn Mercutio against fighting.

Benvolio is not a stick-in-the-mud though, remember, he's the one who suggests they crash the Capulet party!

**TYBALT:**

Tybalt is the nephew to Lady Capulet and therefore a Capulet by marriage, but he seems to have taken on the Capulet cause more zealously than those born into the family. One wonders if Tybalt's motivation may be a desire to take over as head-of-the-family when Capulet dies. With only one daughter, there is no direct heir to Capulet and perhaps Tybalt is constantly trying to prove himself worthy to his uncle.

Tybalt seems to have appointed himself the keeper of the feud and is the greatest troublemaker. He looks for any and all opportunities to take offense at the Montagues and defend the Capulet honor. This is evident in the first scene when he refuses to accept Benvolio's explanation for having his sword drawn among the servants, and insists that they fight. (Note that as soon as Gregory sees Tybalt approaching, he feels it is safe to push the action to another level knowing that Tybalt would never object to them picking a fight with the Montagues and that he'd back them up.)

Tybalt is obsessed with honor and correctness. He is a prig and lives strictly by the book of rules, leaving no leeway for youthful shenanigans. We see this in his behavior at the party. He is totally unwilling to accept Romeo's presence there in spite of his uncle's insistence. He even goes so far as to risk his uncle's fury by insisting that Romeo be made to leave. When Capulet calls Tybalt a "saucy boy" he means that he is an impudent, insolent, conceited young man. His uncle forces him to swallow his anger and endure Romeo's presence which Tybalt must do, for after all, Capulet is still head of the family. Tybalt nurses his grudge and follows up on it the very next day when he sends a challenge to Romeo's house.

Mercutio refers to Tybalt with cat-like images: "king of cats" and "ratcatcher"—this is because the name Tybalt is very similar to *Tybert* which was the name given to a cat in a story "Reynard the Fox", well-known at the time. Note how cat-like Tybalt is, calm, self-assured, but ready to pounce at any moment!

In Tybalt's exchange with Mercutio, we see that Tybalt is nowhere near as clever as Mercutio. His is a mono-maniacal, one-track, aggressive personality, totally lacking in wit or humor. Form and correctness are critical to him as we see in his encounter with Romeo. He is persistent to the extreme and will allow nothing to alter his course of revenge.

**CAPULET:**

Capulet is the head of his family. This means he has final say over the activities of all of his relatives. Financial dealings, marriage proposals, business ventures etc., all must get his approval. He is a man used to respect and to getting his own way—he does not tolerate disobedience as we plainly see in his encounters with Tybalt, Juliet, the Nurse and even with Lady Capulet. The one person he must answer to is the Prince.

Capulet is an older man as indicated by the Prince's reference to him as "old Capulet" and his own reference to himself and Montague as "men so old as we." He has married a much younger woman and Juliet is their only child.

In the very first scene, we see how sensitive he is to the possibility of insult. He comes on ready to fight with Montague even though all Montague is doing is coming on to check out the disturbance just as he himself is doing.

We see him next having returned from his meeting with the Prince. Paris has come to propose a marriage between himself and Juliet. We see Capulet as the older, doting, daddy who would do anything for his little girl. He tells Paris that Juliet is too young to be married. This indulgent, caring father wants to protect his child and keep her with him as long as possible. He is quick to point out that Paris will have to win Juliet's approval before a marriage might even be considered—this was unusual at this time because the father would have absolute control over who and when his daughter would marry—this indulgence on the part of Capulet will, of course, soon change! But now, with everything going smoothly, he can afford to be considerate.

At his feast, we see him at his magnanimous best. Capulet is a rich man and loves to entertain. He welcomes his guests with open arms and even upon discovering that Romeo has crashed the festivities, insists that Tybalt do nothing to disturb his guests.

We have to wonder how Capulet really feels about the annoying young Tybalt. We note how generous he is in his description of Romeo's good qualities—he must know how much this will irritate Tybalt. We also note that in the scene following Tybalt's death, Capulet does not speak a word—it is Lady Capulet who begs for revenge for her nephew's death.

We don't hear from Capulet again until Act 3 scene 4 when Paris has returned to the Capulet house to pay his condolences after Tybalt's death and to find out what Juliet thought of him at the feast the night before. Here we once again see the very concerned father in action.

Three factors are driving him: first, his desire to get Juliet out of the very deep depression she is in—ostensibly over the death of her cousin Tybalt—remember, her parents have no inkling that she has fallen in love with Romeo; secondly, with the death of Tybalt, he realizes that there would be no male heir to take over for him in the case of his own death

and he must tend to this issue by getting an appropriate son-in-law; and thirdly, with the increased enmity between the Capulets and the Montagues caused by this latest fighting, he knows it would be advantageous to have his family allied with the Prince's family by marriage. These are the forces behind his decision to marry Juliet to Paris so hastily.

It is only when Juliet rejects his edict, that we see Capulet as the cranky, stubborn, tyrant who will brook no opposition. He is thoroughly flabbergasted at the notion that his little Juliet would cross him and his anger is extreme as the threats fly at Juliet and he finally delivers his ultimatum and storms out.

But, having ranted and raved, he is quick to forgive Juliet when she returns from Friar Laurence's, an apparently reformed young lady. He is so very delighted with this change-of-heart that he pushes the marriage up a day.

It is not till the end of the play when all his hopes for the future are gone, that we realize what a sad old man he is.

**LADY CAPULET:**

Lady Capulet is much younger than her husband. As she points out to Juliet, she was not much older than Juliet is now when she gave birth to her.

Marriages, among the nobility, were not a matter of love relationships, but of joining together powerful families. The young daughters often paid a high price for their families' successful alliances. Lady Capulet entered into such a marriage for her family and so it is not unusual for her to expect her daughter to do the same.

The relationship between Lady Capulet and her daughter appears to be quite formal—we never see any warmth between them.

We see Lady Capulet at her most passionate after the death of Tybalt. Tybalt is her older brother's son and, assuming Tybalt is about the same age as Romeo and Benvolio, she was about 11 or 12 when he was born and probably thinks of him as a baby brother. She is also particularly partial to Tybalt because she understands that with no other male heirs, Tybalt is likely to take over as head of the family after Capulet's death and this would be beneficial to her as his close relative.

Women at this time were forever subject to the whims and desires of the men who controlled their lives. There was no escaping this system and Lady Capulet knew the advantages of having her own blood relative in charge of her future. This may explain her intense desire for revenge after Tybalt's death.

Once we understand the system that Lady Capulet must exist within, we better understand that she is not the unfeeling mother, (as she is so often portrayed) but a practical woman of her time who knows what must be done in order to survive.

## MONTAGUE:

Montague is somewhat a mirror image of Capulet. He is a gentler, more sensitive version of him and definitely less flamboyant and party-loving.

He is head of his just as powerful family. Romeo is his only son and we see that Montague is a very concerned and caring father. He is most anxious to learn the cause of his son's depression and, as he says, would "willingly give cure."

It is a heartbreaking moment at the end of the play when old Montague comes to the tomb and sees his only son dead and says, "O thou untaught! What manners is in this, to press before thy father to a grave?" We see here all his hopes and dreams dashed, he is a man who has learned his bitter lessons in the hardest possible way.

## LADY MONTAGUE:

Lady Montague is the equally compassionate and caring partner to her husband. More maternal than Lady Capulet—she is perhaps an older woman, more concerned with her children's happiness than her own.

## PRINCE:

The Prince is the ruler of Verona. His word is law and he is the final arbiter on all issues facing the people of his town. He has had enough of the feuding between the families and he wants peace.

The Prince only appears in *Romeo and Juliet* at moments of extreme passion and then to restore the peace and to dispense justice. We see a sense of fairness and benevolence in all his actions towards his subjects.

He is a reasonable man and wisely does not favor either side with his judgments. He is willing to alter his decrees when the situation requires. After having declared, "If ever you disturb our streets again, your lives shall pay the forfeit of the peace," he softens this sentence to exile in Romeo's case, noting the extenuating circumstances.

## PARIS:

Paris is a cousin (meaning, relative) to the Prince and a titled member of the royal family—a count. He is probably a few years older than the other young men in the play which might explain his lack of youthful impetuosity. In any case, his attitude and demeanor set him apart. When Capulet tells him that he must wait two years before marrying Juliet, he seems perfectly willing to do this—imagine if Romeo had been told to wait!

Paris is an extremely proper, very diplomatic young man. We note this in his conversations with Capulet and with Friar Laurence—he always seems to say the correct thing and is careful never to offend.

While he is the perfect husband for Juliet from her parents point of view, we can understand why Juliet herself is not swept off her feet by Paris.

## NURSE:

In wealthy families at this time, it was the custom to have a nurse take care of children from the time they were born until they were old enough to be on their own.

A woman from the lower classes who had recently given birth herself and was therefore capable of breastfeeding the new baby was hired to care for the child.

This is no doubt why Juliet seems to be much closer to the Nurse than she is to her own mother. The relationship between the Nurse and Juliet is much more casual and relaxed—note the ease with which Juliet and the Nurse converse whenever they are alone—very different from the formality of Lady Capulet and Juliet's conversations!

The Nurse is much older than Lady Capulet and is rather *ditzy*. We see this in her first scene with Juliet and Lady Capulet when she babbles on about Juliet's age and later when she meets Romeo in the square. We note too her lack of formal education, while she is definitely a woman of good common sense, she has no book learning and often misinterprets the meanings of words.

The Nurse is extremely protective of Juliet. When she is sent to meet Romeo to inquire about the time and place of the marriage ceremony, she first makes a point of speaking her mind and letting young Romeo know that he mustn't betray her young lady!

We must wonder though why the Nurse, who is well aware of the Capulets' desire to wed Juliet to Paris, offers no objections to Juliet's plan to marry Romeo—in fact she seems to get right into the swing of things, planning the event with Juliet. Perhaps she too finds Paris a bit stuffy and prefers the more daring spirit of Romeo—or is it that the Nurse would do anything to make Juliet happy?

The scene between Juliet and the Nurse after the Nurse has met Romeo is wonderfully playful and comic and again demonstrates the extreme closeness between the two. The Nurse tortures Juliet unmercifully before giving her the information she is so anxiously awaiting. Only someone in a very close and loving relationship could get away with this sort of behavior.

It is only after Tybalt is killed, that we see the self-centered side of the Nurse. She becomes so involved with her own distress, that she almost forgets Juliet's pain and it is not until Juliet is truly in the depths of despair that the Nurse snaps out of it and tends to Juliet.

We then see her wonderfully practical side take charge when she goes to Friar Laurence's to see Romeo. It is the Nurse who finally manages to cut through Romeo's self-indulgent "blubbering and weeping" and says "stand up, an you be a man: for Juliet's sake...rise and stand!" Here she is a no-nonsense lady at her best.

It is the scene when the Nurse tells Juliet to obey her father and marry Paris that gives us pause. We know that the Nurse is well aware of the fact that Juliet is already married to Romeo and that not only would a marriage to Paris be bigamous, but it would mean the ultimate betrayal of Juliet's vows to Romeo. We are forced to wonder about the Nurse's moral standards—is this even an issue for her? Perhaps we are again seeing the practical side of this woman. She believes that any hope for a normal marriage with Romeo has been destroyed by his banishment and that Juliet should get on with her life and find happiness if she can. What the Nurse does not realize is that Juliet has grown up in the last few days. She is no longer the little girl who could be made happy with a new plaything. She is now a young woman who has experienced the love of a young man and she is not about to give him up for anything in the world! It is often difficult for our elders to realize that we have grown up, and in this case, the Nurse's insensitivity to Juliet's new-found maturity causes the split between them.

**FRIAR LAURENCE:**

It was not uncommon at this time for members of the clergy to dabble in the field of medicine. So it is that Friar Laurence collects herbs and flowers and is very knowledgeable about the powers that nature's bounty possesses.

He believes that everything on earth has a purpose no matter how lowly, and that, when used correctly, serves mankind; but when misused—can destroy.

He and Romeo seem to have a special relationship. Friar Laurence is Romeo's mentor and it is to him that Romeo goes when he needs advice. We immediately note that Friar Laurence knew about Rosaline when Romeo's parents and Benvolio were totally unaware of his obsession with her.

Obviously Romeo and the friar have had many conversations about love and ladies in the past as Romeo indicates when he says "thou chid'st me oft for loving Rosaline." Theirs is a casual, easy relationship, as is Juliet's with the Nurse.

It is Friar Laurence's naivete at agreeing to go along with Romeo's plan to marry Juliet that makes us wonder about him. His is a well-intentioned, but perhaps rather innocent view of the world. We must believe that he was truly hopeful that a reconciliation was possible between the two families and that he wanted to be a part of the peace process. Had Tybalt not been killed, perhaps it might have been.

It is in the scene after Tybalt's death that we see the friar at his best. He has allowed his young friend to hide out at the church and has gone off to discover what he can about the Prince's edict. When he returns with the news of banishment, he is unprepared for Romeo's reaction and is momentarily at a loss how to deal with him. Finally though, with prompting from the Nurse, he shakes Romeo out of his self-indulgent wallowing and with a very logical, reasonable and convincing argument gets Romeo to act appropriately.

It is only after Capulet insists on a wedding between Paris and Juliet that we see the friar frantically beginning to unravel. His remedy seems convoluted and irresponsible. We have to wonder whether the friar even considered any of the possible alternatives to the course he chooses. Could he have smuggled Juliet out of Verona and sent her to Romeo and let them deal with the future together? Could he have gone to Capulet and confessed his part of the secret marriage and tried to reason with him?—or is he so afraid of the consequences he might have to face, that he doesn't dare? We have to hope that the friar was acting in good conscience and to the best of his abilities, but we wish that the young lovers had chosen a better advisor!

It is when the friar panics and leaves Juliet in the tomb that we really feel he fails. We can certainly sympathize with his fear, but we cannot forgive him for his cowardice in leaving Juliet—he could at least have carried her away with him. (Of course if he had, the incredibly wonderful and tragic ending of the play would not have been possible—perhaps the friar was as much a victim of Shakespeare's dramatic vision as his own cowardice!)

**MERCUTIO:**

The name Mercutio comes from the word *mercurial* which means changeable, eloquent, ingenious, and cunning: all qualities which Mercutio possesses.

We first hear of Mercutio when Romeo reads the guest list to the Capulet feast—Mercutio and his brother Valentine (who we never see) have been invited. Mercutio is a relative of the Prince and therefore is accepted by both the Capulets and the Montagues.

We finally meet him outside the Capulet house as he, Benvolio and Romeo are preparing to go in.

Mercutio is making fun of Romeo's pining over Rosaline and trying to cajole him out of his serious, romantic mood.

Mercutio is a clever and witty wordsmith. He and Romeo have a wonderful time bantering with each other. They seem to duel with their words–taking each others thoughts and turning them about, parrying, and re-attacking, and thoroughly enjoying each other's whimsy and creativity in the battle.

They are very close friends and Mercutio's kidding of Romeo is offered in this vein. He does not like seeing his pal in pain–especially over a woman. Mercutio himself appears to be quite cynical when it comes to ladies. This can probably be attributed to the fact that his biting wit drives them away and therefore he himself has never had a girlfriend. Romeo's line "he jests at scars that never felt a wound," seems to reinforce this theory.

Another thing we notice about Mercutio is his bawdy sense of humor. We see examples of this both when he "conjures" Romeo by Rosaline's "quivering thigh" and again when he refers to the hand of the clock "upon the prick of noon" when talking to the Nurse. Shakespeare's audience loved those sexual references and Shakespeare often peopled his plays with characters who could satisfy this desire. (In *Romeo and Juliet* Mercutio and the Nurse both salt their language with sexual innuendo. The first scene between Sampson and Gregory is also extremely bawdy. Unfortunately, many of these references have become so obscure that we've had to cut them out of our version. For those of you wishing to explore this further– get out your lexicons and thesauri and check it out!)

Mercutio constantly seems to push things too far. His sense of boundary seems to be very different from that of the average person. We see this after the party when he persists in tormenting Romeo and later in the scene in which he eggs Tybalt on to fight.

Mercutio despises Tybalt! This may be based on the fact that Tybalt hates Romeo and Mercutio is being loyal to his friend or it could be because Mercutio cannot tolerate Tybalt's priggish correctness. In any case there is no love lost between them and Mercutio is ready and anxious to fight with Tybalt.

The opportunity shows itself when Romeo refuses to take up Tybalt's challenge. Mercutio, unaware of Romeo's reason for refusing to fight, takes it upon himself to defend his friend's honor. If only Romeo had not tried to stop the duel all might have been well. Mercutio, as a relative of the Prince, was not subject to the no-fighting edict that the Prince had issued and therefore would have been able to eliminate Tybalt without any repercussions. In trying to part them, Romeo in effect causes Mercutio's death and therefore feels compelled to avenge it by killing Tybalt. Once this happens, there is no hope for Romeo and Juliet's relationship.

**ROMEO:**

Romeo is about sixteen years old, he's smart, rich, good-looking, an excellent swordsman, witty, well-thought of, yet he is miserable! Why?

His dad tells us that he has been moping around and his parents are at their wits' end trying to determine the cause of his depression. His cousin Benvolio has also noticed this and agrees to pursue the issue privately with Romeo.

We soon learn that Romeo is head over heels in love with a girl named Rosaline who wants nothing to do with him–unrequited love–the heartbreak of many a romantic young man and Romeo is miserable to say the least!

Benvolio thinks it would be a good idea if Romeo were to check out other women and he hatches the idea of crashing the Capulet party that night.

The next time we see Romeo, he is still in the dumps. He not only is still pining for Rosaline, but now we learn that he has had an ominous dream. A dream which makes him believe that "some consequence shall...begin with this night's revels" that will end his life! His friends go to great lengths to cheer him up and then drag him to the party.

Once inside, we witness an instantaneous and complete transformation. He sees Juliet Capulet! Now he is in love! This is it! The real thing! And look how he changes! He goes from a mooning, sighing, lovesick boy to a lively, flirting, dashing, daring, man-of-action. When Romeo and Juliet meet some of the finest flirting imaginable passes between them. After those words and those kisses–OOOOOeeeee–he will never be the same!

Having now met the girl of his dreams, Romeo cannot bear to leave Juliet. This daring young fellow risks all for love and climbs the high walls that surround her house and gets the thrill of his life when he overhears her talking to herself about him! He discovers, to his incredible joy, that she loves him back. This previously sulky young man comes into his own. Nothing can stop him now–not the fact that Juliet is a Capulet, not the high walls that surround her, not even the possible threat of death from her angry family if they should find him at her window.

In this second meeting, Romeo is so utterly entranced by Juliet and her sincere love for him that he suddenly finds himself engaged to be married and he couldn't be happier.

Having parted from her, he rushes to his mentor and confidant, Friar Laurence to arrange for a secret marriage.

Upon leaving Friar Laurence's, he runs into Benvolio and Mercutio. They immediately notice the change in him and think that he is his old self again. Mercutio even remarks, "now art thou sociable, not art thou Romeo." What they don't realize is that this is the new Romeo. The Romeo who has met Juliet!

For a few glorious moments, Romeo's life is perfect—he is in love with a wonderful young lady, about to be married to her, the prospect of peace between their families looms entrancingly ahead of him—life could not be better!

The plan seems to be working out perfectly—Juliet appears at the church, the wedding takes place, Romeo has sent his servant to meet the Nurse with a rope ladder that will transport him to Juliet's bedroom. Romeo need only get through the rest of the afternoon and ultimate bliss will be his!

Unfortunately for all concerned, Tybalt exists. His unrelenting quest for revenge will not allow him to rest until he makes Romeo pay for having crashed the Capulet feast.

Imagine Romeo's struggle as he is confronted by Tybalt in the town square—he has just married Juliet and is therefore cousin-by-marriage to Tybalt. Demonstrating amazing self-control, he resists Tybalt's baiting and attempts to leave but Mercutio takes it upon himself to step in and fight his battle for him. Romeo desperately wishes to stop the fighting and in the process of trying to accomplish this, causes Mercutio to be stabbed—the ultimate of ironies!

Romeo's sense of honor now rushes in and overcomes any feelings of sympathy he may have had towards Tybalt and he furiously dispatches him! He has avenged his friend's death, restored his own sense of honor but, in the process, he has destroyed any possibility of happiness for himself and Juliet. He has ruined his life and he knows it! He says, "O I am fortune's fool." Romeo, having so recently been at his peak, is now in the very depths of despair and he once again runs to Friar Laurence.

Romeo is just plain unlucky, he is indeed a "star-crossed lover." Romeo has now realized this and it is more than he can bear. He falls on the floor, "blubbering and weeping" as the Nurse says. She and the Friar then work a near miracle. They teach Romeo what every tragic hero must learn—no matter your mistakes, no matter that everything may conspire against you, you must stand up, square your shoulders and face it. Life is not fair but that can't stop you from trying to do what is right. For Romeo that means that he must love his wife, make sure she is alright, face his banishment and wait for a better day. And you know what?—that is just what he does.

Later, when he learns of Juliet's 'death', (another cruel twist of fate) he knows exactly what he will do.

As he indicated earlier to the friar, he can see no reason to live without Juliet, and now that she is gone—he will join her in death. His determination from this point on in the play is unwavering. This is a profoundly deep love that Romeo and Juliet share, and we wish, with all our hearts, that they could have enjoyed it longer.

**JULIET:**

Juliet is two weeks away from her fourteenth birthday. She is an obedient, well-mannered young girl as we see in her first scene with her mother and her Nurse.

In this scene, Lady Capulet has come to tell her about Paris' interest in her as his bride. Juliet takes the news calmly saying, "It is an honor that I dream not of." Obviously Juliet is not yet obsessed with the idea of boys. But this is about to change!

We next see Juliet with Romeo. The young girl, who hardly uttered a word with her mother in the previous scene, is now displaying a wit and brilliance that clearly shines. She is just as captivated with Romeo as he is with her.

She is an incredibly clever young lady as is demonstrated in her ability to pick up on Romeo's scenario of *saint and pilgrim*. She plays her part with the proper mixture of saintly austerity and feminine coyness encouraging more kisses than Romeo may have been brave enough to dare on his own. It is her line, "then have my lips the sin that they have took?" that causes Romeo to kiss her again to "remove the sin."

These kisses quite literally take her breath away. If Juliet was blase about boys before coming to this party, she is no longer. She has met her "only" love and she knows it!

Juliet cannot stop thinking of Romeo. Once back in her room, she goes to her window to ponder the night's events. But this bright and precocious young girl does not merely moan and sigh over her love, but with impeccable logic, thinks through the obstacles facing her in a relationship with Romeo.

We now watch a thirteen year old girl trying to solve one of the problems that Shakespeare examines in several of his plays—how can men and women find their way through all the morals and manners of a society to establish a genuine relationship? Juliet, in the "what's in a name?" speech, goes a long way towards showing us how to do this.

She sees through all the labels of class or race or whatever that separate us, and goes right to the core of the person, showing that *who* we are and not *what* we are is important. If only the other members of the families could do the same.

Once Juliet realizes that she has been overheard by Romeo, there is nothing coy or flustered about her. She is straightforward with an innocence and honesty that captivates us—she loves and she is not ashamed to admit it. This is a pure heart opening itself. Her only hesitations are for the safety of her beloved and the momentary questioning of the speed of the events.

When the Nurse calls, Juliet must make a decision. The Nurse is calling her back to childhood; Romeo is beckoning her forward into adulthood; her decision is swift and sure, her answer is stunningly beautiful. She says, "all my fortunes at thy foot I'll lay, and follow thee my lord throughout the world."

We must remember the societal restrictions to fully appreciate the daring and impulsiveness of this. Elopement was very uncommon at this time, but even if this were not an issue, Juliet is proposing marriage to the *enemy*, her parents will be livid to say the least. Remember too, that her parents are already discussing Paris as a possible suitor—needless to say, the news of a marriage between a Capulet and a Montague would send shock waves throughout Verona!

But even with all her apparent maturity, remember Juliet is still a child and as such experiences all the desperate impatience of youth. We see this in Act 2 scene 5 as she is awaiting the return of the Nurse with Romeo's instructions. The Nurse is three hours late! Juliet is frantic! Has Romeo changed his mind? has he been talked out of marrying her? can he not find someone to perform the ceremony? and on and on! Juliet's heart is pounding, she has worked herself up into a frenzy of anticipation and anxiety. When the Nurse finally arrives, and gives Juliet the good news, we share her relief.

Once the ceremony has been performed, we find Juliet waiting again—this time the anticipation is so much greater and sweeter—Romeo is coming and they will spend their first night together as husband and wife!

Into this comes the Nurse bringing news of death and banishment. Juliet's world is destroyed. Her momentary doubts towards Romeo—"O serpent heart, hid with a flowering face!"—are quickly dismissed and she is ready to defend her husband to the death, turning on the Nurse when she speaks disparagingly of him. Juliet has faced the first test of marriage—to choose between family or spouse—and she has passed it! Her loyalty to Romeo cannot be questioned.

The next time we see Juliet, she has spent the night with Romeo. But how bitter-sweet is her joy, knowing that this night will be their last for who knows how long.

Juliet must make a bitter journey from the young girl who playfully says "yon light is not daylight" to the mature wife who must look to her husband's safety when she says "it is, it is! Hence be gone, away!"

When Lady Capulet comes in with the news that Juliet must marry Paris on Thursday, what an incredible mix of emotions Juliet must experience—she has just spent the night with the man she loves; parted from him; is miserable, not knowing when she will see him again; and now she is told she must marry someone else!

Juliet's response to the news shocks her parents. They have never seen their little girl act like this before—but, of course, she is no longer that same little girl!

She is a young woman in love. Juliet tries everything to get out of this marriage; she flatly refuses, she pleads with her father on her knees, she begs her mother to help her, she turns to her Nurse—the person who has always stood by her, who helped her marry Romeo—and is told to go along with the marriage to Paris.

Juliet feels totally betrayed by all the people she has depended on in her youth and she emotionally cuts herself off from them. In this desperate state, she goes to the friar, hoping he will have a solution for her.

Juliet believes completely in the sanctity of her marriage vows and her loyalty to Romeo is unimpeachable—she will do anything to remain a faithful wife to her husband.

Juliet accepts the friar's council as her only ray of hope in this dismal affair. She sees no other options and once she receives the vial from the friar along with his instructions, she is committed to her course of action.

Juliet has now learned the same lesson that the friar and the Nurse helped Romeo to learn—namely, that her life is in her own hands and she must face the consequences of her actions wherever that may lead her.

Juliet's commitment is unwavering; her bravery phenomenal; she drinks the potion. When she awakens and discovers the friar's plan to have failed so disastrously, she doesn't hesitate for a moment—she will not live without Romeo!

**FRIAR JOHN:**

Friar John is of the same order as Friar Laurence. He seems to be a helpful, sincere priest, genuinely concerned for the unfortunate.

**WATCHMEN:**

The watchmen can be thought of as policemen on the beat. Their territory is the town of Verona and they are attracted to the cemetery because of Romeo's torch. They have come to investigate the source of the light. They are no-nonsense men and they do their job well.

# "What's in a name?"

### (Juliet: Act 2 scene 2)

| Cast List | abbr.* |
|---|---|
| Chorus | |
| Prince of Verona | Pr |
| Paris, kinsman to the Prince | Par |
| Mercutio, kinsman to the Prince | Mer |
| | |
| Montague, head of his house | Mont |
| Lady Montague, his wife | LaM |
| Romeo, their son | Rom |
| Benvolio, cousin to Romeo | Ben |
| Abram, servant to the Montagues | Ab |
| Balthasar, servant to the Montagues | Balt |
| | |
| Capulet, head of his house | Cap |
| Lady Capulet, his wife | LaC |
| Juliet, their daughter | Jul |
| Tybalt, nephew to Lady Capulet | Tyb |
| Nurse, nurse to Juliet | Nur |
| Sampson, servant to the Capulets | Sam |
| Gregory, servant to the Capulets | Greg |
| | |
| Friar Laurence, a priest | FrL |
| Friar John, a priest | FrJ |
| | |
| Three Watchmen | Watch 1, 2, 3 |

*These are the abbreviations of the characters' names that we have used in the column of stage directions that we have included for those of you wanting blocking suggestions for a production of the play.
[] Bracketed notations that appear throughout the text are interpretive hints that we've included for actors doing either a reading or a production of the play.

## Prologue · scene description

*Romeo and Juliet* begins with an actor delivering a prologue. A prologue is an introductory speech. In the case of *Romeo and Juliet,* the prologue tells us that: two feuding households in Verona have renewed their fighting; that two young people on the opposite sides of the feud will fall in love and die; and that their deaths will cause their parents to make peace.

In effect, the prologue has told us the basic story of the play in addition to telling us how it will end.

## Prologue · vernacular

CHORUS:
Two families—of equal dignity,
living in lovely Verona, where this
play takes place, re-fan the flames
of their past hatred. Born into these
feuding families are two ill-fated lovers;
whose unfortunate and pitiable
deaths will bury their parents' discord.
The dreadful course of their doomed love,
is now the story we are about to tell.

## Act One · Scene 1   scene description

The first characters that we meet are the servants of the two households. Sampson and Gregory are members of the Capulet house. We discover them in the town square, and we quickly realize that they are looking for a fight.

On come two of the Montague servants, Abram and Balthasar, and we see that Abram, at least, is perfectly willing to oblige them.

Into the square, comes Benvolio, who is a Montague, and Tybalt, who is a Capulet. Benvolio tries to stop the fighting; Tybalt, though, instigates a fight with Benvolio.

From opposite sides of the town square, come the patriarchs of the two families. Both are ready to get into the fray, and both of their wives try to hold them back.

We finally have the entrance of the Prince. He, with great effort, gets the attention of the feuding parties and threatens them with death if they ever fight in the streets again.

The Prince then takes Capulet with him, and instructs Montague to come later in the afternoon, to discuss the incident further. Everyone disperses, leaving Montague, Lady Montague and Benvolio.

Montague asks Benvolio for the details of the quarrel, which Benvolio supplies. The conversation then turns to Romeo who has not been seen by his parents all day. Benvolio tells them that he saw Romeo right after sunrise moping around near the woods, but that Romeo made a point of avoiding him and so he did not pursue him.

## Act One · Scene 1   vernacular

SAMPSON:
I often fight when I'm pushed too far.

GREGORY:
But you aren't often pushed far enough
to fight.

SAMPSON:
A dog working for the Montagues is
pushing my buttons.

GREGORY:
Get ready; here come two of Montague's
men.

SAMPSON:
My bare blade is out; you start, I'll
cover your back.

GREGORY:
What? You'll turn your back and run?

SAMPSON:
Fear me not. Let's make sure the law's
on our side; let them start.

GREGORY:
I'll stare them down as we walk by
and let's see what they do.

SAMPSON:
No. I'll give them the finger—let's
see if they'll put up with that.

| Prologue **original abridged** | Prologue **stage directions** |
|---|---|

**CHORUS:**
Two households, both alike in dignity,
in fair Verona, where we lay our scene,
from ancient grudge, break to new mutiny.
From forth the fatal loins of these two foes,
a pair of star-crossed lovers take their life;
whose misadventured piteous overthrows
doth, with their death, bury their parents' strife.
The fearful passage of their death-marked love,
is now the two hours traffic of our stage.

*(enter UC X C)*

*(exit UC)*

| Act One • Scene 1 **original abridged** | Act One • Scene 1 **stage directions** |
|---|---|

**SAMPSON:**
I strike quickly, being moved.

*(Sam & Greg enter DL, Sam has his sword out and is fighting an imaginary opponent, Sam X C displaying 'skill', Greg stays DL watching him)*

**GREGORY:**
But thou art not quickly moved to strike.

**SAMPSON:**
A dog of the house of Montague moves me.

*(brandishing sword toward Montague house, starting to put sword away)*

**GREGORY:**
Draw; here comes two of the house of Montagues.

*(looking in direction of Montague house)*

**SAMPSON:**
My naked weapon is out; quarrel, I will back thee.

*(draws sword and scurries DL behind Greg)*

**GREGORY:**
How? Turn thy back and run?

*(turning to Sam)*

**SAMPSON:**
Fear me not. Let us have the law on our side; let them begin.

**GREGORY:**
I will frown as I pass by, and let them take it as they list.

**SAMPSON:**
Nay, I will bite my thumb at them, which is a disgrace to them if they bear it.

*(demonstrating thumb-bite\*)*

## Act One · Scene 1   scene description

*Continued*

   Montague says that Romeo seems quite depressed these days and that he is concerned and does not know the cause.
   Seeing Romeo approach, Benvolio suggests that they leave him alone with Romeo and that he will try to discover the reason for his depression.
   Benvolio quickly figures out that unrequited love is the cause, and suggests to Romeo that the best way to get over a woman, is to find another lady. Romeo rejects this idea, but Benvolio insists it will work and they go off together, continuing this conversation.

## Act One · Scene 1   vernacular

*[enter Abram and Balthasar]*

ABRAM:
Are you shooting us the finger, sir?

SAMPSON:
I'm shooting the finger, sir.

ABRAM:
Are you shooting the finger at *us*, sir?

SAMPSON: *[to Gregory]*
Would a judge be on our side, if I say yes?

GREGORY:
Nope.

SAMPSON:
Nope, I'm not shooting the finger at
you, sir; but I am shooting the finger, sir.

GREGORY:
You looking for trouble, sir?

ABRAM:
Trouble, sir? No, sir!

SAMPSON:
Cause if you are, sir, I'm ready; we
Capulets are as good as you Montagues.

ABRAM:
Only "as good?"

SAMPSON:
Well, sir.

GREGORY: *[to Sampson]*
Say—better; here comes one of the
bosses' cousins.

SAMPSON:
Yeah, better, sir.

ABRAM:
You lie.

| Act One·Scene 1  **original abridged** | Act One·Scene 1   **stage directions** |
|---|---|
| *[enter Abram and Balthasar]* | *(enter UR xing RC, as Sam moves C, biting his thumb, Ab is L of Balt)* |
| ABRAM:<br>Do you bite your thumb at us, sir? | |
| SAMPSON:<br>I do bite my thumb, sir. | *(stopping LC still biting his thumb)* |
| ABRAM:<br>Do you bite your thumb at *us,* sir? | |
| SAMPSON: *[to Gregory]*<br>Is the law on our side, if I say—ay? | *(x DL to Greg and whisper)* |
| GREGORY:<br>No. | |
| SAMPSON:<br>No sir, I do not bite my thumb at you, sir; but I bite my thumb, sir. | *(xing to Ab & Balt, biting his thumb)* |
| GREGORY:<br>Do you quarrel, sir? | *(xing between Sam and Ab)* |
| ABRAM:<br>Quarrel, sir? No, sir. | |
| SAMPSON:<br>But if you do, sir, I am for you; I serve as good a man as you. | *(over Greg shoulder)* |
| ABRAM:<br>No better! | |
| SAMPSON:<br>Well, sir. | |
| GREGORY: *[to Sampson]*<br>Say—better; here comes one of my masters' kinsmen. | *(glancing off DL, seeing Tyb in the distance, whispers to Sam)* |
| SAMPSON:<br>Yes, better, sir. | *(glancing offstage DL)* |
| ABRAM:<br>You lie. | |

**Act One • Scene 1**                    **vernacular**

SAMPSON:
Fight, if you got the guts. *[they fight]*

BENVOLIO: *[entering]*
Stop it, you fools; put away your swords;
you don't know what you're doing.

*[enter Tybalt with his sword out]*
TYBALT:
What, are you fighting with these
lily-livers? Turn around Benvolio,
face your death.

BENVOLIO:
I'm only trying to keep peace; put away
the blade, or use it to help me break this up.

TYBALT:
What! blade out and talking of peace?
I hate that word as much as I hate hell,
all Montagues, and you. Take that coward!

*[Capulet, Lady Capulet, Montague and
Lady Montague enter]*
CAPULET:
What's all this racket? My sword!

LADY CAPULET:
What do you want with your sword?

CAPULET:
My sword! Old Montague is coming with
his sword out, to spite me.

MONTAGUE:
Capulet, you villain!—Leave me alone,
let go of me.

LADY MONTAGUE:
You're not moving a foot to get in a
fight.

PRINCE: *[enters]*
Rebellious citizens, disturbers of the
peace, listen to me! What's this! you
men, you beasts,—on pain of torture,
throw your weapons to the ground and

SAMPSON:
Draw, if you be men. *[they fight]*

BENVOLIO: *[entering]*
Part fools; put up your swords; you
know not what you do.

*[enter Tybalt with his sword drawn]*
TYBALT:
What, art thou drawn among these
heartless hinds? Turn thee Benvolio,
look upon thy death.

BENVOLIO:
I do but keep the peace; put up thy
sword, or manage it to part these men with me.

TYBALT:
What, drawn, and talk of peace? I hate
the word, as I hate hell, all Montagues,
and thee. Have at thee, coward!

*[Capulet, Lady Capulet, Montague and Lady
Montague enter]*
CAPULET:
What noise is this? My sword!

LADY CAPULET:
Why call you for a sword?

CAPULET:
My sword, I say! Old Montague is come,
and flourishes his blade in spite of me.

MONTAGUE:
Thou villain, Capulet!—Hold me not, let
me go.

LADY MONTAGUE:
Thou shalt not stir one foot to seek a
foe.

PRINCE: *[entering]*
Rebellious subjects, enemies to peace,
will they not hear? What, ho! you men,
you beasts,—on pain of torture, throw
your weapons to the ground and hear the

*(fight\*)*

*(enter UR, draw sword, cross
US of the fighting, with
sword motion from ground
upwards, tries to separate
their swords-they back off
a bit-as Tyb enters DL,
sword drawn, xing DLC)*

*(x DRC opposite Tyb)*

*(lunges at Ben, they fight\*,
servants cheer them on)*
*(Cap & LaC from DL, Mont
with sword from UR, LaM
pulling on his arm)*
*(from DL)*

*(yelling offstage DL)*

*(in UR corner, brandishing
sword in Cap direction,
trying to shake loose of
LaM)*

*(enters UC, says first line)*

*(xing C, all part)*

hear the sentence of your furious prince.
*[they drop their weapons and listen]*
Three brawls, started by you, old
Capulet and Montague, have three times
now, disturbed our quiet streets. If
you ever disturb the peace again, you'll
pay for it with your lives. Capulet,
you go with me, and Montague, you come
this afternoon to know the rest of what
I have to say about this. Once again,
on pain of death, everyone clear out.
*[all exit except Benvolio, Montague
and Lady Montague]*

MONTAGUE:
Who began the old feud all over again?
Tell me nephew, were you here when
it started?

BENVOLIO:
Your servants, and those of your foe,
were fighting when I came. I drew my
sword to try to part them; but at that
moment, came hot-headed Tybalt, with
his sword already out. While we were
fighting, the prince came, who broke
it all up.

LADY MONTAGUE:
Oh, where is Romeo? Have you seen him
today? I'm so glad he wasn't part of this fray.

BENVOLIO:
Madam, an hour before sunrise,
I saw your son; I started towards him;
but when he saw me, he took off into
the woods. I, figuring he needed
to be alone, willingly, let him be.

MONTAGUE:
This isn't the first time he's been
seen there, adding the wetness of his tears
to the morning's dew.

BENVOLIO:
My noble uncle, do you know the cause of this?

sentence of your moved prince.
*[they all drop their weapons and listen]*
Three brawls, bred by thee, old Capulet
and Montague, have thrice disturbed the
quiet of our streets. If ever you
disturb our streets again, your lives
shall pay the forfeit of the peace.
You, Capulet, shall go along with me,
and Montague, come you this afternoon
to know our farther pleasure in this
case. Once more, on pain of death, all
men depart.*[all exit except Benvolio,
Montague and Lady Montague]*

MONTAGUE:
Who set this ancient quarrel new abroach?
Speak nephew, were you by, when it
began?

BENVOLIO:
Here were the servants of your adversary,
and yours, fighting ere I did approach.
I drew to part them; in the instant came
the fiery Tybalt, with his sword prepared.
While we were interchanging thrusts and
blows, the prince came, who parted either
part.

LADY MONTAGUE:
O, where is Romeo! Saw you him today?
Right glad am I, he was not at this fray.

BENVOLIO:
Madam, an hour before the sun peered
forth the golden window of the east,
did I see your son; towards him I made;
but he was 'ware of me, and stole into
the covert of the wood. I measuring his
affections by my own, gladly shunned
who gladly fled from me.

MONTAGUE:
Many a morning hath he there been seen,
with tears augmenting the fresh morning's dew.

BENVOLIO:
My noble uncle, do you know the cause?

*(drop weapons, Caps move
DL with Cap DL of Pr, Monts
move DR with Mont DR of
Pr, the ladies DR & DL
of their husbands, nephews
next, servants in DR & DL
corners)*

*(Pr exits UC, Cap and rest
of Caps exit DL, Balt &
Ab exit UR)*

*(turning to Ben)*

*(x to between Mont & LaM
as Mont and LaM counter\*)*

MONTAGUE:
I neither know it, nor can find it out
from him.

BENVOLIO:
Have you tried to get it out of him?

MONTAGUE:
Yes, myself and through friends.
But he is so secretive. If we could only
learn the cause of his sorrow, we would
willingly try to cure it.

BENVOLIO:
Look, he's coming. If you don't mind,
leave us alone; and I'll find out what's
bothering him.

MONTAGUE:
Come madam, let's go. *[they exit]*

BENVOLIO:
Good morning, cousin.

ROMEO:
Is it still just morning?

BENVOLIO:
It's just 9 A.M.

ROMEO:
Oh my! sadness makes the time crawl
by. *[changing the subject]* Was that
my father who just ran off?

BENVOLIO:
It was.—What sadness makes your day
seem so long?

ROMEO:
Not having that—which if I had—would
make my day seem short.

BENVOLIO: *[figuring out Romeo's riddle]*
Oh, in love?

| Act One·Scene 1 **original abridged** | Act One·Scene 1 **stage directions** |
|---|---|

MONTAGUE:
I neither know it, nor can learn of
him.

BENVOLIO:
Have you importuned him by any mean?

MONTAGUE:
Both by myself, and many other friends.
But he is to himself so secret and so close.
Could we but learn from whence his sorrows
grow, we would as willingly give cure.

BENVOLIO:
See, where he comes. So please you, step
aside; I'll know his grievance.

*(seeing Rom offstage DR)*

MONTAGUE:
Come, madam, let's away. *[they exit]*

*(hurry off UR)*

BENVOLIO:
Good morrow, cousin.

*(x to Rom as Rom enters
DR)*

ROMEO:
Is the day so young?

BENVOLIO:
But new struck nine.

ROMEO:
Ay me? sad hours seem long. *[changing
the subject]* Was that my father that
went hence so fast?

*(x DRC, looking off UR)*

BENVOLIO:
It was.–What sadness lengthens Romeo's
hours?

ROMEO:
Not having that–which having–makes
them short.

BENVOLIO: *[figuring out Romeo's riddle]*
In love?

*(x to Rom)*

**Act One • Scene 1**                    **vernacular**

ROMEO:
Out–!

BENVOLIO:
Of love?

ROMEO:
Out of favor, with the one I love.

BENVOLIO:
Oh dear, that love, who appears so sweet, should be so cruel and rough.

ROMEO:
Oh my!–was there a fight? No, don't tell me, I know all about it. Besides, I've got my own problems, farewell.

BENVOLIO:
Tell me, sad one, who are you in love with?

ROMEO:
Sadly, cousin, I do love a woman.

BENVOLIO:
I figured as much, when I thought you were in love.

ROMEO:
But, she won't be hit with Cupid's arrow. She swears she will not love; and that vow, kills me dead even though I'm alive to say it.

BENVOLIO:
Take my advice: forget her.

ROMEO:
Oh, and how do you suggest I do that?

BENVOLIO:
Check out other pretty faces.

| Act One·Scene 1 **original abridged** | Act One·Scene 1 **stage directions** |
| --- | --- |

ROMEO:
Out–!

BENVOLIO:
Of love?

ROMEO:
Out of her favor, where I am in love.

BENVOLIO:
Alas, that love, so gentle in his view,
should be so tyrannous and rough.

ROMEO:
Oh me!–What fray was here? Yet tell
me not, for I have heard it all. Griefs
of mine own lie heavy in my breast,
farewell.

*(x C, noticing weapons on ground)*

BENVOLIO:
Tell me in sadness, who is that you love?

*(x RC pursuing Rom)*

ROMEO:
In sadness, cousin, I do love a woman.

BENVOLIO:
I aimed so near, when I supposed you
loved.

ROMEO:
Well, she'll not be hit with Cupid's
arrow. She hath forsworn love; and in
that vow, do I live dead, that live to
tell it now.

BENVOLIO:
Be ruled by me, forget to think of her.

ROMEO:
Oh, teach me how I should forget.

BENVOLIO:
By giving liberty unto thine eyes; examine
other beauties.

## Act One • Scene 1    vernacular

ROMEO:
Goodbye. You're a big help!

BENVOLIO:
I'll make you forget her, or else I'll
die trying. *[both exit]*

## Act One • Scene 2    scene description

This scene takes place at the front door of the Capulet house, with Capulet telling count Paris about the Prince's rulings regarding the street brawl. Paris then asks Capulet if he would consider allowing him to marry Juliet.

Capulet tells Paris that he believes Juliet is too young to marry and that it would be two years before he thinks she would be old enough. Paris points out that there are young women in Verona even younger than Juliet who already have children.

Capulet doesn't approve of these young marriages, but he does agree to allow Paris to court Juliet. He tells him though, that Juliet's input in the matter is critical to his decision.

Capulet invites Paris to come to a feast that he is planning for the evening. He then sends Sampson with a guest list to invite the rest of the people.

It is immediately obvious that Sampson is unable to read, and needs assistance. At that moment Romeo and Benvolio enter, still engrossed in their conversation about women.

Romeo, after a bit of joking, reads the list to Sampson, and then asks where the people are to go. Sampson tells him about the Capulet feast and goes off to carry out his errand.

Benvolio, having noted that Rosaline—Romeo's unrequited love—has been invited, suggests that they go to the party so that Romeo will be able to see his love in contrast to other beautiful women, and will hopefully fall out of love with her. Romeo agrees to go, but only in order to see Rosaline.

## Act One • Scene 2    vernacular

*[enter Capulet and Paris]*
CAPULET:
Montague must obey the law the same
as I; and truly it shouldn't be hard
I think, for men as old as we are to
keep the peace.

PARIS:
You are both honorable and it's a pity
you have been at odds for so long. But
now sir, what do you think of my proposal
to seek your daughter's hand in marriage?

CAPULET:
My child is still an innocent, she is
not even fourteen yet. You'll have to
wait two more years before I'd let her
marry you.

PARIS:
Girls younger than she are already mothers.

CAPULET:
Being made a mother so young is never
good. All my other children have died,
she is my only one. But court her gentle
Paris, win her affection; my approval
is along with her consent what you'll need.
Tonight I'm giving a dinner, and I've invited
many guests, and you would be most
welcome. *[calling]* You there!
*[to Sampson]* Go around Verona,
and find the people whose names are

## Act One · Scene 1  **original abridged**

ROMEO:
Farewell, thou canst not teach me to forget.

BENVOLIO:
I'll pay that doctrine, or else die in
debt. *[both exit]*

## Act One · Scene 1    **stage directions**

*(Rom starts off UL)*

*(following Rom)*

*(exit UL, as Samp & Greg enter DL,
Ab & Balt enter UR, clear weapons
and exit where they entered)*

## Act One · Scene 2  **original abridged**

*[enter Capulet and Paris]*
CAPULET:
Montague is bound as well as I; in
penalty alike; and 'tis not hard, I think,
for men so old as we to keep the peace.

PARIS:
Of honorable reckoning are you both, and
pity 'tis you lived at odds so long. But
now, my lord, what say you to my suit?

CAPULET:
My child is yet a stranger in the world,
she hath not seen the change of fourteen
years; let two more summers wither in
their pride ere we may think her ripe to
be a bride.

PARIS:
Younger than she are happy mothers made.

CAPULET:
And too soon marred are those so early
made. The earth hath swallowed all
my hopes but she. But woo her, gentle
Paris, get her heart, my will to her
consent is but a part. This night I
hold a feast whereto I have invited
many a guest, and you among the store,
one more, most welcome. *[calling]*
Sirrah! *[to Sampson]* Trudge about
through fair Verona, find those persons out,

## Act One · Scene 2    **stage directions**

*(enter UC, walking slowly
DS as they talk)*

*(stopping C to talk more)*

*(continue walking DL)*

*(calls offstage DL)*
*(Sam enters DL, Cap hands
him guest list)*

written there. Tell them we're having
a party at which we'd like them to
appear. *[Paris and Capulet exit]*

SAMPSON:
Find them out! Whose names are written
here? I must to the learned.

BENVOLIO:
Come on man, one fire will extinguish
another, just as a new pain makes an
old one go away; so take a new lady
and put her in your eye and the memory
of the old one will soon die.

SAMPSON:
Good day.—Excuse me sir, can you read?

ROMEO:
Yes, if I know the letters and the language.

SAMPSON: *[having no idea what Romeo
means]*
Ah, right; see you!

ROMEO:
Come back, man, I can read.
*[reading the list]*
"Signior Martino, and his wife and
daughter; County Anselme and his
beauteous sisters; Signior Placentio,
and his lovely nieces; Mercutio, and
his brother Valentine; my uncle Capulet,
his wife and daughters; my fair niece
Rosaline; Livia; Signior Valentio, and
his cousin Tybalt." A nice group;
where should they come?

SAMPSON:
Up.

ROMEO:
Where?

SAMPSON:
To our house.

| Act One · Scene 2 **original abridged** | Act One · Scene 2 **stage directions** |
|---|---|

whose names are written there, and
to them say, my house and welcome on
their pleasure stay. *[Paris and Capulet exit]*

*(exit DL)*

SAMPSON:
Find them out, whose names are written
here? I must to the learned.

*(turning paper all around, he obviously can't read, looks around, sees Ben & Rom entering UL xing UR, still in conversation)*

BENVOLIO:
Tut man! One fire burns out another's
burning, one pain is lessened by another's
anguish; take thou some new infection to
thy eye, and the rank poison of the old
will die.

SAMPSON:
Good den.—I pray sir, can you read?

*(x to them)*

ROMEO:
Ay, if I know the letters and the language.

SAMPSON: *[having no idea what Romeo means]*
Ye say honestly; rest you merry!

*(starts to go DR)*

ROMEO:
Stay, fellow, I can read.
*[reading the list]*
"Signior Martino, and his wife and
daughter; County Anselme, and his beauteous
sisters; Signior Placentio, and his lovely
nieces; Mercutio, and his brother Valentine;
mine uncle Capulet, his wife and daughters;
my fair niece Rosaline; Livia; Signior
Valentio, and his cousin Tybalt." A fair
assembly; Whither should they come?

*(Sam x to Rom and hands him paper)*

*(hands paper back to Sam)*

SAMPSON:
Up.

ROMEO:
Whither?

SAMPSON:
To our house.

## Act One · Scene 2    vernacular

ROMEO:
Whose house?

SAMPSON:
My master's—the great rich Capulet,
and if you aren't a Montague, come drink
some wine with us. See you. *[he exits]*

BENVOLIO:
At this very feast, dines that lovely
Rosaline, who you love so. Go to it,
and compare her face with some that
I will show, and I'll make you see that
your swan is a crow.

ROMEO:
All right, I'll go, but no such sight
will I see, for only Rosaline has beauty
for me. *[they exit]*

## Act One · Scene 3    scene description

We now switch to the interior of the Capulet house.

Lady Capulet is asking the Nurse to call Juliet to her. Juliet appears and, after a bit of banter about Juliet's age, Lady Capulet begins a discussion of marriage with Juliet and informs her that count Paris has expressed interest in her. The Nurse finds this news tremendously exciting, while Juliet takes it more calmly and agrees to consider the count.

Sampson then appears with the news that the guests are beginning to arrive.

## Act One · Scene 3    vernacular

*[enter Lady Capulet and Nurse]*
LADY CAPULET:
Nurse, where's my daughter? Call her to me.

NURSE:
Lamb! Ladybird! *[no response]*
Where is that girl? *[shouting]* Juliet!

JULIET: *[entering]*
What is it? Who wants me?

NURSE:
Your mother.

JULIET:
Madam, I'm here. What is it you want?

LADY CAPULET:
This is the substance of it—*[to Nurse]* you
know that my daughter is approaching maturity.

NURSE:
Truly, I know exactly how old she is.

| **Act One · Scene 2  original abridged** | **Act One · Scene 2  stage directions** |
| --- | --- |

ROMEO:
Whose house?

SAMPSON:
My master's; the great rich Capulet; and
if you be not of the house of Montagues,
I pray you come and crush a cup of wine.
Rest you merry. *[he exits]*

*(exits DR)*

BENVOLIO:
At this same feast, sups the fair Rosaline
whom thou so lovest. Go thither; and
compare her face with some that I shall
show, and I will make thee think thy swan
a crow.

ROMEO:
I'll go along, no such sight to be
shown, but to rejoice in splendor of
mine own. *[they exit]*

*(exit UR)*

| **Act One · Scene 3  original abridged** | **Act One · Scene 3  stage directions** |
| --- | --- |

*[enter Lady Capulet and Nurse]*
LADY CAPULET:
Nurse, where's my daughter? Call her to me.

*(Greg enters UL with stool which he
places LC then x UL, bows to LaC as
she enters UL with Nur, Greg exits UL,
LaC x to stool and sit)*

NURSE:
What, lamb! What, ladybird! *[no response]*
Where is this girl? *[shouting]* What, Juliet!

*(Nur x SL, calls off SL)*

JULIET: *[entering]*
How now? Who calls?

*(enter SL)*

NURSE:
Your mother.

JULIET:
Madam, I am here. What is your will?

*(x to LaC)*

LADY CAPULET:
This is the matter–*[to Nurse]* thou
knowest, my daughter's of a pretty age.

NURSE:
'Faith, I can tell her age unto an hour.

*(xing in a little)*

**Act One • Scene 3          vernacular**

LADY CAPULET:
She's almost fourteen.

NURSE:
I'll bet fourteen of my teeth—and
yet, I only have four—she's not
fourteen. How long is it till Lammas-tide?

LADY CAPULET:
Two weeks and some odd days.

NURSE:
Well even or odd, of all the days of
the year, she will be fourteen the night
of Lammas-tide. I remember well—*[going
off on a tangent]* it is eleven years
since the earthquake and she was weaned
—I never shall forget it...

LADY CAPULET: *[interrupting]*
Enough of this: I beg you, be quiet.

NURSE:
My lips are sealed!

LADY CAPULET:
Tell me, daughter Juliet, what are your
thoughts about marriage?

JULIET:
It's not something that I've thought
much about.

LADY CAPULET:
Well think about it now. Girls younger
than you, here in Verona, respectable
young ladies, are already mothers. By
my count, I was already your mother,
when I was your age. Briefly then, the
worthy gentleman, Paris would like you
for his wife.

NURSE:
Oh, he's a handsome one, young lady,
quite a catch!

**Act One·Scene 3   original abridged**

**Act One·Scene 3   stage directions**

LADY CAPULET:
She's not fourteen.

NURSE:
I'll lay fourteen of my teeth—and yet,
I have but four—she's not fourteen. How
long is it now to Lammas-tide?

LADY CAPULET:
A fortnight and odd days.

NURSE:
Even or odd, of all the days in the year,
come Lammas-tide at night, she shall be
fourteen. I remember it well. *[drifting
off on a tangent]* 'Tis since the earthquake now eleven years; and she was
weaned—I never shall forget it—

*(turning DS, off in her own
world)*

LADY CAPULET: *[interrupting]*
Enough of this: I pray thee, hold thy peace.

NURSE:
Peace, I have done!

*(turning back to LaC)*

LADY CAPULET:
Tell me, daughter Juliet, how stands
your disposition to be married?

JULIET:
It is an honor that I dream not of.

LADY CAPULET:
Well think of marriage now. Younger
than you, here in Verona, ladies of
esteem, are made already mothers. By my
count, I was your mother much upon these
years that you are now a maid. Thus then,
in brief, the valiant Paris seeks you
for his love.

NURSE:
A man, young lady! Such a man.

*(excited, xing in a little more)*

## Act One · Scene 3                    vernacular

LADY CAPULET:
What do you say? Do you think you could love him? He'll be at our banquet tonight? Look him over as you would a book and see how charmingly his tale has been written. Tell me, do you like this idea?

JULIET:
I'll consider it, but go no further than you think is correct.

GREGORY: *[excited]*
Madam, the guests are arriving.

LADY CAPULET:
We'll be right there.—Juliet, the count is waiting. *[they all exit]*

## Act One · Scene 4  scene description

The scene now shifts to the town square, in front of the Capulet house. Mercutio, who has been invited to the Capulet party, is there with his two friends, Romeo and Benvolio, who were not invited, but are planning to *crash* the party.

They all have masks which they will put on to go into the house. This was a custom which allowed young men and women to flirt somewhat anonymously, so the fact of their appearing this way does not arouse suspicion.

Romeo is reluctant to go but Benvolio encourages him, saying that they will merely dance a bit and then leave. Romeo, still depressed about Rosaline, insists he will not dance and he and Mercutio get into a discussion about the cruelty of love.

They are just about to enter when Romeo hesitates saying that it is unwise to go in and blames his reluctance on a dream he has had. Mercutio attributes the dream to Queen Mab who he says makes lovers dream of love.

Romeo tells them of his premonition that something that begins at the party tonight will end his life! But he shakes this off and goes on into the Capulet house.

## Act One · Scene 4                    vernacular

*[enter Romeo, Benvolio and Mercutio]*
ROMEO:
What, shall we just go on in?

BENVOLIO:
We'll dance one dance and then leave.

ROMEO:
I don't feel like dancing; I'm depressed.

MERCUTIO:
No, gentle Romeo, you must dance.

ROMEO:
Not me, believe me; I'm so depressed, I couldn't move.

MERCUTIO:
You're a lover; strap on Cupid's wings and fly with them.

ROMEO:
I'm too wounded from his arrow, to fly with his feathers.

## Act One · Scene 3  **original abridged**

**LADY CAPULET:**
What say you? Can you love the gentleman? This night you shall behold him
at our feast. Read o'er the volume of
young Paris' face, and find delight
writ there with beauty's pen. Speak
briefly, can you like of Paris' love?

**JULIET:**
I'll look to like, but no more than your
consent gives strength.

**GREGORY:** *[excited]*
Madam, the guests are come.

**LADY CAPULET:**
We follow thee.—Juliet, the county
stays. *[they all exit]*

## Act One · Scene 4  **original abridged**

*[enter Romeo, Benvolio and Mercutio]*
**ROMEO:**
What, shall we on?

**BENVOLIO:**
We'll measure a measure, and be gone.

**ROMEO:**
I am not for this ambling, being but heavy.

**MERCUTIO:**
Nay, gentle Romeo, we must have you dance.

**ROMEO:**
Not I, believe me; I have a soul of lead,
I cannot move.

**MERCUTIO:**
You are a lover; borrow Cupid's wings,
and soar with them.

**ROMEO:**
I am too sore empierced with his shaft,
to soar with his light feathers.

## Act One · Scene 3  **stage directions**

*(runs in from UL)*

*(exit UL, Greg takes stool)*

## Act One · Scene 4  **stage directions**

*(enter UR xing towards C,
Ben has masks, Rom stops)*

*(they play this scene in
the UR diagonal part of
stage, create movement
as needed, these are three
close friends on their way
to a party—have fun!)*

## Act One · Scene 4    scene description

*Continued*

Capulet welcomes the masked young men and instructs the music and dancing to begin.

Romeo sees Juliet for the first time as she is dancing and is immediately entranced with her beauty and decides that he must seek her out following the dance and, at the very least, touch her hand.

Tybalt, having recognized Romeo's voice, is furious that Romeo should have come into the Capulet party. Capulet tries to get Tybalt to calm down by saying that he has heard good things about Romeo. This infuriates Tybalt further and Capulet finally has to resort to threats upon his nephew in order to keep the peace in his home.

We now see Romeo and Juliet's first meeting. Romeo, wearing his mask, approaches Juliet in the guise of a religious pilgrim seeking the blessing of a saint. Juliet picks up immediately on the game and goes along with it brilliantly. They each take on their respective parts and play them to the hilt until they manage to artfully exchange three thrilling kisses and the rest, as they say, is history!

The Nurse interrupts with the message that Lady Capulet wishes to see Juliet. While she is gone, Romeo discovers Juliet's identity.

The party is now breaking up and as Romeo is leaving, Juliet learns that Romeo is a Montague.

## Act One · Scene 4    vernacular

MERCUTIO: *[ironically]*
Love!—a tender thing!

ROMEO:
Is love a tender thing? It is rough, and rude, and boisterous; and it pricks like thorns.

MERCUTIO:
If love is rough on you, be rough on love; prick love back, beat it down. Give me my mask.

BENVOLIO:
Come on, knock, and enter; and as soon as we're in, everybody dance.

ROMEO:
This is stupid.

MERCUTIO:
Why, may one ask?

ROMEO:
I dreamt a dream last night.

MERCUTIO:
And so did I.

ROMEO:
Well, what was yours?

MERCUTIO:
That dreamers often lie.

ROMEO:
That they do—they lie in bed, asleep, while they dream things that are true.

MERCUTIO:
Oh, then I see Queen Mab has visited you. She is the fairies' midwife, and appears no larger than a tiny stone. And in this form she gallops night after night through lovers' brains and makes them dream of love.

MERCUTIO: *[ironically]*
Love!—a tender thing!

ROMEO:
Is love a tender thing? It is too rough,
too rude, too boisterous; and it pricks
like thorn.

MERCUTIO:
If love be rough with you, be rough with
love; prick love for pricking, beat love
down! Give me a case to put my visage in.

*(Ben hands out masks)*

BENVOLIO:
Come, knock, and enter; and no sooner in,
but every man betake him to his legs.

ROMEO:
'Tis no wit to go.

MERCUTIO:
Why, may one ask?

ROMEO:
I dreamt a dream tonight.

MERCUTIO:
And so did I.

ROMEO:
Well, what was yours?

MERCUTIO:
That dreamers often lie.

ROMEO:
In bed, asleep, while they do dream
things true.

MERCUTIO:
O, then I see Queen Mab hath been with
you. She is the fairies' midwife, and
she comes in shape no bigger than an
agate stone and in this state she gallops
night be night through lovers' brains
and then they dream of love.

ROMEO:
Easy, easy, Mercutio, easy; you're
talking nonsense.

MERCUTIO:
True, I'm talking about dreams; which
are the product of an unproductive brain,
bred from frivolous fantasies.

BENVOLIO:
They've finished supper, I'm afraid
we'll be too late.

ROMEO:
I'm afraid, too early: I have an odd
premonition. Something that will happen
tonight, will begin the end of my life.
*[shaking off this premonition]* But God,
who guides me, lead me on!—On lusty
gentlemen.

CAPULET:
You are welcome, gentlemen! Come on,
let's have some music—dance, girls.

ROMEO: *[talking to himself]*
Who is that young lady? She sparkles
brighter than the candlelight! When
the dance is over, I'll watch where
she goes to rest, and touching her hand,
make my hand blest. Was I ever in love
before tonight? I only thought I loved
before seeing this sight. *[exit]*

TYBALT: *[who has overheard Romeo]*
That is the voice of a Montague!
Now, by my family's honor, to kill him,
is no sin.

CAPULET: *[seeing how worked up Tybalt is]*
What's the matter? Why are you storming
around so?

TYBALT:
Uncle, he's a Montague, our enemy; who
has come to spite us.

## Act One·Scene 4 **original abridged**

ROMEO:
Peace, peace, Mercutio, peace; thou
talk'st of nothing.

MERCUTIO:
True, I talk of dreams; which are the
children of an idle brain, begot of
nothing but vain fantasy.

BENVOLIO:
Supper is done and we shall come too late.

ROMEO:
I fear, too early: for my mind misgives.
Some consequence shall bitterly begin with
this night's revels, and expire the term
of life, closed in my breast. *[shaking
off this premonition]* But He, that hath
the steerage of my course, direct my
sail!—On lusty gentlemen.

*(put on their masks, Mer stamps his foot
3 times C stage)*

CAPULET:
You are welcome, gentlemen! Come musicians,
play—foot it, girls.

*(Cap enters from DL, greets them and
leads them off DL into the party,
Rom hangs back, stopping and looking
off DL into party where music is playing\*)*

ROMEO: *[talking to himself]*
What lady's that? O, she doth teach the
torches to burn bright! The measure done,
I'll watch her place of stand, and,
touching hers, make blessed my rude hand.
Did my heart love till now? Forswear it,
sight! For I ne'er saw true beauty till
this night. *[exit]*

*(Tyb has entered DR, stands
listening to Rom)*
*(exits DL)*

TYBALT: *[who has overheard Romeo]*
This, by his voice, should be a Montague!
Now, by the stock and honor of my kin, to
strike him dead, I hold it not a sin.

*(xing L and pulling out his
sword)*

CAPULET: *[seeing how worked up Tybalt is]*
Why, how now. Wherefore storm you so?

*(Cap enters DL, hearing the
end of Tyb's line)*

TYBALT:
Uncle, this is a Montague, our foe; that
is hither come in spite.

CAPULET:
Young Romeo, is it?

TYBALT:
It's him, that villain Romeo.

CAPULET:
Take it easy, kind cousin, leave him
alone. He's acting like a gentleman;
and, to be honest, the whole town says
that he is a virtuous and well-mannered
young man. Therefore be patient, pay
him no mind.

TYBALT:
I won't stand for it.

CAPULET:
You will stand for it. Is this my house
or yours? Watch it!—you won't stand
for it!—God, help me—you'll cause
a mutiny among my guests!

TYBALT: *[protesting]*
But, Uncle...

CAPULET: *[angrily]*
Watch it, watch it, you're an insolent
boy—shut up or I'll shut you up! *[exit]*

TYBALT: *[aside*]*
I'll back down: and though I will appear
sweet now, I will make him pay somehow.
*[exits]*

ROMEO:
If I offend your gentle hand with the
rough touch of mine, I am prepared to
kiss away that roughness with my lips.

JULIET:
You needn't apologize for your hand,
even saints have hands that pilgrims'
hands touch, and a handshake would suit
even the holiest.

| Act One • Scene 4 **original abridged** | Act One • Scene 4 **stage directions** |
|---|---|

**CAPULET:**
Young Romeo is't?

**TYBALT:**
'Tis he, that villain Romeo.

**CAPULET:**
Content thee, gentle coz, let him alone.
He bears him like a gentleman; and, to
say truth, Verona brags of him, to be a
virtuous and well-governed youth. Therefore be patient, take no note of him.

**TYBALT:**
I'll not endure him.                                         *(attempting to pass Cap and*
                                                            *exit DL)*

**CAPULET:**
He shall be endured. Am I the master here,                  *(Cap, blocking Tyb's way,*
or you? go to, you'll not endure him!—                      *getting angrier as he goes*
God, mend my soul—you'll make a mutiny                      *on)*
among my guests!

**TYBALT:** *[protesting]*
Why, uncle...

**CAPULET:** *[angrily]*
Go to, go to, you are a saucy boy—be
quiet or I'll make you quiet! *[exits]*                      *(exits DL)*

**TYBALT:** *[aside*]*
I will withdraw: but this intrusion shall,
now seeming sweet, convert to bitter gall.
*[exits]*                                                   *(exits SL)*

**ROMEO:**                                                  *(Jul enters DL xing DC,*
If I profane with my unworthiest hand                       *cooling off after dance,*
this holy shrine, my lips, ready stand                      *Rom follows her on, kneels*
to smooth that rough touch with a tender kiss.              *to her and takes her hand)*

**JULIET:**
You do wrong your hand too much. For
saints have hands that pilgrims' hands
do touch, and palm to palm is holy
palmers' kiss.

ROMEO:
Don't saints have lips?

JULIET:
Yes, pilgrim. Lips that they use to
pray.

ROMEO:
O then, dear saint, let lips do what
hands do.

JULIET:
Saints do not move.

ROMEO:
Then don't move while I receive the
fruit of my prayer. *[he kisses her]*
Now your lips have purged my lips of their sin.

JULIET:
Then is the sin on my lips now?

ROMEO: *[coyly]*
The sin from my lips? I'll take it back
again. *[he kisses her again]*

JULIET:
You kiss too politely. *[she kisses him
more passionately]*

NURSE: *[entering]*
Miss, your mother wants to talk to you.
*[Juliet exits]*

ROMEO: *[to Nurse]*
Who is her mother?

NURSE:
To be sure, her mother is the lady of
the house.

ROMEO: *[aside]*
Is she a Capulet? Oh dear, my enemy!

| Act One·Scene 4 **original abridged** | Act One·Scene 4    **stage directions** |
|---|---|
| ROMEO:<br>Have not saints lips? | |
| JULIET:<br>Ay, pilgrim, lips that they must use in<br>prayer. | |
| ROMEO:<br>O then, dear saint, let lips do what<br>hands do. | *(raising up his mask)* |
| JULIET:<br>Saints do not move. | |
| ROMEO:<br>Then move not, while my prayer's effect<br>I take. *[kisses her]* Thus from my lips,<br>by thine, my sin is purged. | *(stands and kisses her gently)* |
| JULIET:<br>Then have my lips the sin that they have<br>took? | |
| ROMEO: *[coyly]*<br>Sin from my lips? Give me my sin again. | *(he kisses her again)* |
| JULIET:<br>You kiss by the book. *[she kisses him<br>more passionately]* | *(she kisses him)* |
| NURSE: *[entering]*<br>Madam, your mother craves a word with<br>you. *[Juliet exits]* | *(enters DL)*<br><br>*(Jul runs off DL)* |
| ROMEO: *[to Nurse]*<br>What is her mother? | *(x to Nur)* |
| NURSE:<br>Marry, her mother is the lady of<br>the house. | |
| ROMEO: *[aside]*<br>Is she a Capulet? O dear, my foe! | *(x to DC)* |

## Act One · Scene 4                    vernacular

BENVOLIO: *[entering]*
Let's go; the party's starting to fade.

ROMEO:
Yes, I'm afraid it is.

JULIET: *[reenters]*
Nurse, who is that gentleman—the one
going out the door?

NURSE:
I don't know.

JULIET:
Go ask his name.

NURSE:
His name is Romeo and he is a Montague;
the only son of your great enemy.

JULIET:
My only love, born of my only hate!
I didn't know when I saw him and now
it's too late!

NURSE:
What's that—what's that?

JULIET:
A little poem I just learned.

NURSE:
The guests have left; come, let's go
too. *[they exit]*

## Act Two · Scene 1  scene description

The scene begins with Romeo sneaking back to Juliet's. Benvolio and Mercutio try to find him, but Romeo is hiding and they eventually give up and leave.

## Act Two · Scene 1                    vernacular

ROMEO: *[enters]*
Can I leave, when the one I love is
here? I must go back and find my heart.

BENVOLIO: *[calling]*
Romeo! my cousin Romeo! Romeo!

## Act One · Scene 4    **original abridged**

BENVOLIO: *[entering]*
Away, begone; the sport is at the best.

ROMEO:
Ay, so I fear; the more is my unrest.

JULIET: *[reenters]*
Nurse, what is yon gentleman—he that
now is going out of door?

NURSE:
I know not.

JULIET:
Go ask his name.

NURSE:
His name is Romeo and a Montague; the
only son of your great enemy.

JULIET:
My only love, sprung from my only hate!
Too early seen unknown and known too
late!

NURSE:
What's this—what's this?

JULIET:
A rhyme I learned even now.

NURSE:
Come, let's away; the strangers all are
gone. *[they exit]*

## Act One · Scene 4    **stage directions**

*(running in from DL, x to Rom, Mer
enters with him but runs in a circle
around Nur before joining Ben and Rom)*

*(Ben, Rom and Mer move C)*

*(enters DL, whispers to Nur)*

*(Nur x to Ben, whispers,
he quickly whispers back)*

*(x to Jul, whisper, Mer &
Ben drag Rom off UR as Rom
watches Jul)*

*(turning DS)*

*(turning back to Nur)*

*(Nur pulls Jul off SL)*

## Act Two · Scene 1    **original abridged**

ROMEO: *[enters]*
Can I go forward, when my heart is here?
Turn back, and find thy center out.

BENVOLIO: *[calling]*
Romeo! my cousin Romeo! Romeo!

## Act Two · Scene 1    **stage directions**

*(Greg & Sam bring on ladder UL, as Rom
place it LC on the diagonal, exit UL
runs on DR, stops, looks off DR)*

*(Ben & Mer play scene in DR corner
and stay just offstage, when Rom hears
them, he hides under ladder)*

**Act Two • Scene 1                    vernacular**

MERCUTIO:
He's a bright boy; and I swear, he's already gone home to bed.

BENVOLIO:
He ran this way. Call, good Mercutio.

MERCUTIO:
Romeo! wacko! lover-boy! *[no response]* He doesn't hear, he doesn't respond, he doesn't move; the ape is dead! I'll bring him back.—I conjure you by Rosaline's bright eyes, by her dainty foot, and her quivering thigh!

BENVOLIO:
If he hears you, he'll be angry.

MERCUTIO:
My invocation is fair and honest.

BENVOLIO:
Come on, he's hidden himself.

MERCUTIO:
Romeo, good night. *[to Benvolio]* Come, shall we go? *[they exit]*

**Act Two • Scene 2  scene description**

Juliet, who has gone up to her bedroom, comes to her window and Romeo sees her there. Romeo compares her presence to the amazing beauty and power of a sunrise.

She finally speaks and what she says thrills Romeo beyond belief. She is bemoaning the fact that the man she has fallen in love with is a member of the Montague family and determines that it is merely his name that is her enemy and if he would give up his name, they could be together.

Romeo, unable to contain his joy, speaks out and agrees to her bargain. Juliet is stunned, having thought she was alone, but after a moment of

**Act Two • Scene 2                    vernacular**

ROMEO:
He makes fun of feelings he's never felt. *[sees Juliet at the window]* But hush! What is that vision in the window there? It is dawn and Juliet is the sun! It is my lady! Oh, it is my love! *[Juliet is talking to herself—we don't hear what she is saying]* She's speaking, but I can't hear what she's saying; I will speak. *[stops himself]* I am too bold, she's not speaking to me. Look how she leans her cheek on her hand! I wish I could be a glove on that hand so that I might touch her cheek!

## Act Two · Scene 1  **original abridged**

**MERCUTIO:**
He is wise; and on my life, hath
stolen him home to bed.

**BENVOLIO:**
He ran this way. Call, good Mercutio.

**MERCUTIO:**
Romeo! madman! lover! *[no response]* He
heareth not, he stirreth not, he moveth
not; the ape is dead! I must conjure him.–
I conjure thee by Rosaline's bright eyes,
by her fine foot, and quivering thigh!

**BENVOLIO:**
An if he hear thee, thou wilt anger him.

**MERCUTIO:**
My invocation is fair and honest.

**BENVOLIO:**
Come, he hath hid himself.

**MERCUTIO:**
Romeo, good night. *[to Benvolio]* Come,
shall we go? *[they exit]*

## Act Two · Scene 1  **stage directions**

*(they walk up along R side of stage
and exit UR, while Jul enters UL x to
ladder and climbs up, as Rom comes
out from under ladder and x C)*

## Act Two · Scene 2  **original abridged**

**ROMEO:**
He jests at scars that never felt a
wound. *[sees Juliet at the window]* But
soft! What light through yonder window
breaks? It is the east and Juliet is the
sun! It is my lady: O it is my love!
*[Juliet is talking to herself—we don't
hear what she is saying]* She speaks, yet
she says nothing; I will answer. *[stops
himself]* I am too bold, 'tis not to me she
speaks. See how she leans her cheek upon
her hand! O, that I were a glove upon that
hand, that I might touch that cheek!

## Act Two · Scene 2  **stage directions**

*(crouches at SR foot of
ladder, watching Jul)*

## Act Two · Scene 2   scene description

*Continued*

confusion realizes that Romeo could be in great danger if found near her bedroom window.

Romeo insists that the only danger he is in, is the possibility of Juliet rejecting him. Romeo then declares his love for her. Juliet, overwhelmed by the suddenness of it all, and no doubt confused by the rush of feeling she is experiencing, bids Romeo "goodnight."

Romeo wants more—at least a declaration of her love. Juliet points out that she gave that before she even knew he was there. At that moment, we hear the Nurse calling for Juliet.

In the next frenzied moments, with Romeo outside her window and the Nurse calling from within, Juliet takes a giant leap and declares that if Romeo is really serious about his love, they should marry!

Tearing back and forth between the Nurse and Romeo, Juliet arranges a plan for Romeo to get word to her about where and at what time they should marry. She says further, that if he is not serious about marrying her, he should end his courtship immediately! In other words, for Juliet, her incredibly strong feelings towards Romeo can only end in one way—with marriage!

Romeo starts to respond but Juliet, spurred by the need to get back to the Nurse and perhaps a bit embarrassed at her brazen proposal, cuts him off with her line, "A thousand times good night!" and she starts to leave but is immediately drawn back to him and calls for Romeo.

They draw out their parting, enjoying the incredible sweetness of the moment and then separate.

## Act Two · Scene 2   vernacular

JULIET: *[sighing]*
Oh dear!

ROMEO:
She speaks. Oh, speak again, beautiful angel! for you are as glorious as an angel from heaven.

JULIET: *[talking to herself]*
Oh, Romeo, Romeo! Why do you have to be Romeo? Deny your family and give up your name; or, if you won't do that, swear that you love me, and I'll give up mine.

ROMEO: *[aside]*
Should I listen to more or shall I speak?

JULIET:
It is your name that my family hates. You are yourself though, not a Montague. What's Montague? It is not a hand, nor a foot, nor any other part of a man. Oh, be another name! What is a name? The thing we call a rose, called by another name would still smell as sweet. So would Romeo, if he weren't called Romeo, be as perfect as he is, without that name:—Romeo, give up your name; and in exchange for it, take me.

ROMEO:
I take you at your word: just call me your love, and I'll take a new name; from now on I won't be Romeo.

JULIET:
Who are you?

ROMEO:
By a name, I don't know how to tell you who I am. My name, dear saint, is hateful to me, because it is your enemy.

JULIET:
Aren't you Romeo? A Montague?

| | |
|---|---|
| Act Two · Scene 2  **original abridged** | Act Two · Scene 2  **stage directions** |

JULIET: *[sighing]*
Ah me!

ROMEO:
She speaks. O, speak again, bright angel!
for thou art as glorious as is a winged
messenger of heaven.

JULIET: *[talking to herself]*
O Romeo, Romeo! Wherefore art thou Romeo?
Deny thy father and refuse thy name; or, if
thou wilt not, be but sworn my love, and
I'll no longer be a Capulet.

ROMEO: *[aside]*
Shall I hear more or shall I speak?

JULIET:
'Tis but thy name that is my enemy. Thou
art thyself though, not a Montague. What's
Montague? It is nor hand, nor foot, nor
arm, nor face, nor any other part belonging
to a man. O, be some other name!
What's in a name? That which we call a
rose, by any other name would smell as
sweet. So Romeo would, were he not Romeo
called, retain that dear perfection
which he owes, without that title:—
Romeo, doff thy name; and for that name,
which is no part of thee, take all myself.

ROMEO:
I take thee at thy word: call me but
love, and I'll be new baptized; henceforth
I never will be Romeo.

*(stands x RC)*

JULIET:
What man art thou?

*(shocked to hear a voice)*

ROMEO:
By a name, I know not how to tell thee
who I am. My name, dear saint, is hateful
to myself, because it is an enemy to thee.

JULIET:
Art thou not Romeo, and a Montague?

*(straining to see in the dark)*

**Act Two · Scene 2**                    **vernacular**

ROMEO:
I am neither, lovely lady if either
you don't like.

JULIET:
How did you get here?

ROMEO:
With the aid of Cupid's wings.

JULIET:
If any of my family find you here, they
will murder you.

ROMEO:
Oh dear! There is more danger in your
eyes than in twenty of their swords;
if only you will look kindly at me,
I am safe from their hate.

JULIET:
By whose direction did you find this
place?

ROMEO:
Love directed me.

JULIET:
Oh kind Romeo, if you do love me, say
so truthfully.

ROMEO:
Lady, by the blessed moon, I swear...

JULIET: *[interrupting him]*
Oh, don't swear on the moon,—it is
too changeable,—your love might prove
to be changeable too.

ROMEO:
What shall I swear by?

JULIET:
Don't swear at all; this is all too,
rash, too sudden;—sweet, good night!

Act Two·Scene 2 **original abridged**

Act Two·Scene 2   **stage directions**

ROMEO:
Neither, fair maid, if either thee
dislike.

JULIET:
How cam'st thou hither?

ROMEO:
With love's light wings.

JULIET:
If any of my kinsmen find thee here, they
will murder thee.

ROMEO:
Alack! There lies more peril in thine eye,
than twenty of their swords; look thou
but sweet, and I am proof against their
enmity.

JULIET:
By whose direction found'st thou out
this place?

ROMEO:
By love!

JULIET:
O gentle Romeo, if thou dost love,
pronounce it faithfully.

ROMEO:
Lady, by yonder blessed moon, I vow...

JULIET: *[interrupting him]*
O, swear not by the moon, the inconstant
moon, lest that thy love prove likewise
variable.

ROMEO:
What shall I swear by?

JULIET:
Do not swear at all; this is too rash,
too sudden;—sweet, good night!

*(starting to descend)*

ROMEO:
Oh, will you leave me so unsatisfied?

JULIET:
What satisfaction could you have tonight?

ROMEO:
The exchange of your declaration of
love for mine.

JULIET:
I gave you that before you asked for
it—*[Nurse is heard calling, "Juliet"]*
I hear a noise; dear love, adieu. *[Nurse
calls again]* In a minute, Nurse! Sweet
Montague, stay for a moment, I will
return again.

ROMEO:
Oh blessed, blessed night! I'm afraid
this is all just a dream.

JULIET: *[returning]*
Romeo, if you truly love me, and mean
to marry me, send me a message tomorrow,
through the person I will send to you,
telling me where and at what time the
ceremony will be performed; and my
destiny, I will place in your hands, and
follow you, my lord, throughout the world—

NURSE: *[from inside]*
Madam!

JULIET: *[calling offstage to Nurse]*
I'm coming. *[to Romeo]*—but, if your
intentions aren't pure, I beg you,—

NURSE: *[calling, more impatiently]*
Madam!

JULIET: *[to Nurse]*
In a minute: *[back to Romeo]*—to
pursue me no further, and leave me to
my misery. Tomorrow I'll send to you.

| Act Two·Scene 2 **original abridged** | Act Two·Scene 2 **stage directions** |
|---|---|

ROMEO:
O, wilt thou leave me so unsatisfied?

*(xing and grabbing ladder)*

JULIET:
What satisfaction canst thou have tonight?

ROMEO:
The exchange of thy love's faithful vow
for mine.

JULIET:
I gave thee mine before thou didst
request it *[Nurse is heard calling,*
*"Juliet"]* I hear some noise within; dear
love, adieu. *[Nurse calls again]* Anon,
good nurse! *[to Romeo]* Sweet Montague,
stay but a little, I will come again.

*(Nur calls from offstage*
*UL)*

*(descends ladder, exit UL)*

ROMEO:
O blessed, blessed night! I am afeard,
all this is but a dream.

*(leaning against ladder)*

JULIET: *[returning]*
Dear Romeo, if thy love be honorable, thy
purpose marriage, send me word tomorrow,
by one that I'll procure to come to thee,
where and what time thou wilt perform the
rite; and all my fortunes at thy foot
I'll lay, and follow thee my lord
throughout the world—

*(enter UL, climb ladder)*

NURSE: *[calling, from offstage]*
Madam!

*(calls from offstage UL)*

JULIET: *[calling offstage to Nurse]*
I come, anon. *[to Romeo]*—but, if thou
mean'st not well, I do beseech thee,—

NURSE: *[calling, more impatiently]*
Madam!

JULIET: *[to Nurse]*
By and by, I come: *[back to Romeo]*—to
cease thy suit, and leave me to my grief.
Tomorrow will I send.

## Act Two · Scene 2 — vernacular

ROMEO:
For that, my soul lives,—

JULIET:
A thousand times good night!
Romeo!

ROMEO:
What my dear?

JULIET:
What time tomorrow, should I send my messenger?

ROMEO:
By nine o'clock.

JULIET:
I will not fail; it will seem like twenty years till then, good night, good night! Parting is such sweet sorrow, that I shall say good night, till it be tomorrow.

ROMEO:
Sleep come to your eyes, peace to your breast!—I wish I were sleep and peace, and could have so fine a rest! *[both exit]*

## Act Two · Scene 3 — scene description

This scene opens with Friar Laurence collecting medicinal herbs and musing about the good and evil inherent in all things including mankind.

Romeo, having come straight from Juliet, greets the friar, who, noting how early Romeo is up and around, guesses that Romeo has been up all night and wonders if he has been with Rosaline. Romeo quickly dismisses the notion of Rosaline and reveals that he has fallen in love with Juliet and wants the friar to marry them.

The friar, recovering from his initial shock at this sudden change in Romeo's affections, agrees, hoping that such an alliance will bring about a peaceful resolution of the feuding between their families.

## Act Two · Scene 3 — vernacular

*[Friar Laurence enters]*
FRIAR LAURENCE:
The grey-tinged morning is taking the place of night. Before the sun gets too hot, I must fill my basket with deadly weeds, and curative flowers. Oh, great is the power, that these plants and herbs possess. For there is nothing on earth that can't be put to good use, nor nothing so perfect, that if misused, will not cause abuse. These two opposing forces exist in men as well as in herbs —good and ill will—and where the worser quality is predominant, death will soon result.

| Act Two·Scene 2 **original abridged** | Act Two·Scene 2 **stage directions** |
|---|---|

ROMEO:
So thrive my soul,—

JULIET:
A thousand times good night!
Romeo!

ROMEO:
My dear!

*(descends one step, returns)*

JULIET:
What o'clock tomorrow shall I send to
thee?

ROMEO:
By the hour of nine.

JULIET:
I will not fail; 'tis twenty years till
then. Good night, good night! Parting
is such sweet sorrow, that I shall say
good night, till it be morrow.

ROMEO:
Sleep dwell upon thine eyes, peace in
thy breast!—would I were sleep and
peace, so sweet to rest. *[both exit]*

*(Jul exits UL, Rom exits DR, Greg
& Sam enter UL, take ladder off UL)*

| Act Two·Scene 3 **original abridged** | Act Two·Scene 3 **stage directions** |
|---|---|

*[Friar Laurence enters]*
FRIAR LAURENCE:
The grey-eyed morn smiles on the frowning
night. Now ere the sun advance his burning
eye, I must fill this cage with baleful weeds,
and precious-juiced flowers. O mickle is the
powerful grace, that lies in plants and herbs.
For nought so vile that on the earth
doth live, but to the earth some special
good doth give; nor aught so good, but,
strained from that fair use, revolts from
true birth, stumbling on abuse. Two such
opposed kings encamp them still in man
as well as herbs,—grace and rude will;
and, where the worser is predominant,
full soon the canker death eats up that plant.

*(enters SR, carrying basket
of herbs and flowers
surveying the morning,
he delivers his monologue\*)*

*(xing DRC)*

**Act Two · Scene 3**                **vernacular**

ROMEO: *[entering]*
Good morning, father.

FRIAR LAURENCE:
Blessings! Whose sweet voice greets
me so early? Young man, the early hour
suggests you're in some kind of trouble;
if not—and I guess right—Romeo never
went to bed last night.

ROMEO:
That last guess is true, a better time
was mine.

FRIAR LAURENCE:
God forgive your sin! Were you with Rosaline?

ROMEO:
With Rosaline? No; I have forgotten
that name, and all of that pain.

FRIAR LAURENCE:
That's my good boy: but then where have
you been?

ROMEO:
I have been dining with my enemy.

FRIAR LAURENCE:
Be clear, good son.

ROMEO:
Then clearly know, my heart is set on
the fair daughter of Capulet. When,
and where, and how we met, we wooed,
and became engaged, I'll tell you as
we walk; but this I beg of you as we
go on our way, that you will consent
to join us in marriage today.

FRIAR LAURENCE:
Holy Saint Francis! What has happened!
Is Rosaline, whom you did love so dearly,
so soon forgotten?

ROMEO: *[entering]*                                    *(enters SR x to FrL)*
Good morrow, father.

FRIAR LAURENCE:
Benedicite! What early tongue so sweet
saluteth me? Young son, thy earliness doth
me assure, thou art up-roused with some
distemperature; or, if not so, then here
I hit it right—our Romeo hath not been
in bed tonight.

ROMEO:
That last is true, the sweeter rest was
mine.

FRIAR LAURENCE:
God pardon sin! Wast thou with Rosaline?

ROMEO:
With Rosaline? No; I have forgot that
name, and that name's woe.

FRIAR LAURENCE:
That's my good son: but where hast thou
been then?

ROMEO:
I have been feasting with mine enemy.

FRIAR LAURENCE:
Be plain, good son.

ROMEO:
Then plainly know, my heart's dear love
is set on the fair daughter of Capulet.
When, and where, and how we met, we woo'd,
and made exchange of vow, I'll tell thee
as we pass; but this I pray, that thou
consent to marry us today.

FRIAR LAURENCE:                                        *(backing upstage a little)*
Holy Saint Francis! What a change is here!
Is Rosaline, that thou dids't love so dear,
so soon forsaken?

## Act Two · Scene 3    vernacular

ROMEO:
You've scolded me often for loving Rosaline.

FRIAR LAURENCE:
For foolish fondness, not for loving, my pupil.

ROMEO:
I beg you not to scold me. The one I love now, loves me back; the other did not.

FRIAR LAURENCE:
Come, young fickle one, come go with me, for this reason I'll to this agree; this union may turn out well in the end, and turn your feuding families, into friends. *[they exit]*

## Act Two · Scene 4    scene description

We now switch back to the town square where Benvolio and Mercutio are discussing Romeo's whereabouts. Benvolio tells Mercutio that Romeo didn't come home last night and that Tybalt has sent a letter to the Montague house. Mercutio concludes that the letter is a challenge to a duel.

Romeo then comes on so joyfully (remember, he is just coming from the friar's who has agreed to perform the marriage ceremony) that Mercutio thinks Romeo is cured of his love-sickness.

On comes the Nurse in search of Romeo. She asks to speak to him alone and the others depart. After a bit of confusion, during which the Nurse warns Romeo to be true to Juliet, Romeo tells the Nurse that the friar will marry Juliet and him in the church this afternoon.

Romeo also gives the Nurse instructions about a rope ladder which he will use to climb up to Juliet's bedroom that night.

## Act Two · Scene 4    vernacular

*[enter Benvolio and Mercutio]*
MERCUTIO:
Where the devil is Romeo? Didn't he come home last night?

BENVOLIO:
Not to his father's house. Tybalt, the Capulet, sent a letter to his father's.

MERCUTIO:
A dare, I'll bet.

BENVOLIO:
And Romeo will answer it.

MERCUTIO:
Any man, who can write, may answer a letter.

BENVOLIO:
No, he will answer the letter's writer howsoever he dares him.

## Act Two · Scene 3  **original abridged**

ROMEO:
Thou chid'st me oft for loving Rosaline.

FRIAR LAURENCE:
For doting, not for loving, pupil mine.

ROMEO:
I pray thee, chide not. She whom I love
now, doth love for love allow; the other
did not so.

FRIAR LAURENCE:
O come, young waverer, come go with me,
in one respect I'll thy assistant be; for
this alliance may so happy prove, to turn
your households' rancor to pure love.
[they exit]

## Act Two · Scene 3  **stage directions**

*(giving in)*

*(exit SR)*

## Act Two · Scene 4  **original abridged**

[enter Benvolio and Mercutio]
MERCUTIO:
Where the devil should this Romeo be?
Came he not home tonight?

BENVOLIO:
Not to his father's. Tybalt, the kinsman
to old Capulet, hath sent a letter to his
father's house.

MERCUTIO:
A challenge, on my life.

BENVOLIO:
Romeo will answer it.

MERCUTIO:
Any man, that can write, may answer a
letter.

BENVOLIO:
Nay, he will answer the letter's
master how he dares.

## Act Two · Scene 4  **stage directions**

*(enter UC x C as they
speak, play scene C)*

*(pretending to duel with
imaginary sword)*

**Act Two·Scene 4          vernacular**

MERCUTIO:
Oh dear, poor Romeo is already dead;
he's been pierced through his ear-drum
with a love-song! And is he
the man to fight Tybalt?

BENVOLIO:
Why, what's so special about Tybalt?

MERCUTIO:
He's more than just an alley cat. Oh,
he's the duke of deception—a priggish,
affected, phony jerk—may his lips
rot off!

BENVOLIO:
Here comes Romeo. *[Romeo enters]*

MERCUTIO:
Signior Romeo, bonjour! You played a
heck of a trick on us last night.

ROMEO:
Good morning to you both, what trick
did I play?

MERCUTIO:
The slip, sir, you gave us the slip.

ROMEO: *[with a coy grin]*
Pardon me, good Mercutio, but I had
important business, and in such a case,
to hell with manners! *[all three laugh
together enjoying the suggestion that
Romeo has met someone new]*

MERCUTIO: *[happy for Romeo's good mood]*
Why isn't this better than moaning about
love? Now you're fit to be around, now
you're the Romeo we know.

ROMEO: *[seeing Nurse enter]*
Here's someone to be reckoned with!

NURSE: *[enters]*
God grant you good morning, gentlemen.

| Act Two·Scene 4 **original abridged** | Act Two·Scene 4 **stage directions** |
|---|---|

MERCUTIO:
Alas, poor Romeo, he is already dead;
run through the ear with a love-song!
And is he a man to encounter Tybalt?

BENVOLIO:
Why, what is Tybalt?

MERCUTIO:
More than prince of cats I can tell you.      *(imitating Tyb's priggishness,*
Oh, he's the courageous captain of           *basically, making fun of*
compliments. A pox on such antic,           *him)*
lisping, affecting fantasticoes—

BENVOLIO:
Here comes Romeo. *[Romeo enters]*           *(Rom enters SR, x to them)*

MERCUTIO:
Signior Romeo, bonjour! You gave us the
counterfeit fairly last night.

ROMEO:
Good morrow to you both; what counterfeit
did I give you?

MERCUTIO:
The slip, sir, the slip.

ROMEO: *[with a coy grin]*
Pardon, good Mercutio, my business was
great; and in such a case as mine, a
man may strain courtesy. *[all three
laugh together, enjoying the suggestion
that Romeo met someone new]*

MERCUTIO: *[happy for Romeo's good mood]*
Why, is not this better than groaning
for love? Now art thou sociable, now
art thou Romeo.

ROMEO: *[seeing Nurse enter]*                *(Nur enters DL, waving to*
Here's goodly gear!                          *them)*

NURSE:
God ye good morrow, gentlemen.

**Act Two · Scene 4**          **vernacular**

MERCUTIO:
God grant you good afternoon, fair
gentlewoman.

NURSE:
Is it afternoon?

MERCUTIO:
It is, I tell you; for the clock's hand
is on the lascivious prick of noon.

NURSE:
Away with you! Who do you think you are?

ROMEO:
Someone, gentlewoman, who God made to
ruin himself.

NURSE:
I swear, well said;—to ruin himself!
Gentleman, can you tell me where I may
find young Romeo?

ROMEO:
I can tell you. I am the youngest of that
name.

NURSE:
Sir, I desire a word with you.

MERCUTIO:
A madam, a madam! *[Nurse threatens
Mercutio]* Will you come to your father's
house? We're going to dinner there?

ROMEO:
I'll be there in a while.

MERCUTIO:
Farewell, old lady; farewell. *[Mercutio
and Benvolio exit]*

NURSE:
I ask you sir, what foul-mouthed fellow
was that?

| Act Two·Scene 4 **original abridged** | Act Two·Scene 4 **stage directions** |
| --- | --- |

MERCUTIO:
God ye good den, fair
gentlewoman.

NURSE:
Is it good den?

*(xing in a little to them)*

MERCUTIO:
'Tis no less, I tell you; for the bawdy
hand of the dial is now upon the
prick of noon.

*(xing to Nur)*

NURSE:
Out upon you! What a man are you?

*(shoves Mer)*

ROMEO:
One, gentlewoman, that God hath made,
for himself to mar.

*(x between Nur and Mer)*

NURSE:
By my troth, it is well said;—for
himself to mar! Gentlemen, can you tell
me where I may find the young Romeo?

ROMEO:
I can tell you. I am the youngest of that
name.

NURSE:
Sir, I desire some confidence with you.

*(taking his arm, pulls him
DL, whispering to him)*

MERCUTIO:
A bawd, a bawd! *[Nurse threatens Mercutio]*
Romeo, will you come to your father's?
We'll to dinner thither.

*(Nur turns threatening on
Mer, Mer raises his hands
in mock surrender)*

ROMEO:
I will follow you.

MERCUTIO:
Farewell, ancient lady; farewell.
*[Mercutio and Benvolio exit]*

*(exit UR)*

NURSE:
I pray you sir, what saucy merchant was
this?

**Act Two · Scene 4**        **vernacular**

ROMEO:
He's a gentleman, Nurse, who loves to
hear himself talk!

NURSE:
If he says anything against me, I'll
cut him down to size—even if he were
lustier than he is! *[recovering her
composure]* Now sir, a word. My young
lady sent me to find you; what she asked
me to say, I will keep to myself: but
first let me tell you, if you plan to
double-cross her, it would be an evil thing.

ROMEO:
Nurse, my best to your lady. I declare
to you,—

NURSE: *[interrupting]*
Good soul! Truly, I will tell her that:
Lord, lord, she will be a joyful woman.

ROMEO:
What will you tell her, Nurse? you didn't
let me finish.

NURSE:
I will tell her, sir,—that you
declare—which, as I understand, is
a very gentlemanly thing.

ROMEO: *[getting on with things]*
Ask her to find some way to come to
confession this afternoon; there, at
Friar Laurence's she shall be married.
Here's something for your trouble.

NURSE:
No, truly sir—not a penny.

ROMEO:
Come on—I say take it.

NURSE:
This afternoon, sir? Well, she shall
be there.

| Act Two · Scene 4 **original abridged** | Act Two · Scene 4   **stage directions** |
|---|---|

ROMEO:
A gentleman, Nurse, that loves to hear
himself talk!

NURSE:
An' a speak anything against me, I'll                    *(x C looking UR where*
take him down an' a were lustier than he               *Mer has exited)*
is! *[recovering her composure]* Now sir,               *(turning back to Rom)*
a word. My young lady bid me inquire
you out; what she bid me say, I will
keep to myself: but first let me tell
ye, if you should deal double with her,
it were an ill thing.

ROMEO:
Nurse, commend me to thy lady. I protest
unto thee,–

NURSE: *[interrupting]*                                 *(xing to him)*
Good heart! In faith, I will tell her as much:
Lord, lord, she will be a joyful woman.

ROMEO:
What wilt thou tell her, nurse? Thou dost
not mark me.

NURSE:
I will tell her, sir,–that you do
protest–which, as I take it, is a
gentlemanlike offer.

ROMEO: *[getting on with things]*
Bid her devise some means to come to               *(speaking confidentially*
shrift this afternoon; there she shall              *to Nur)*
at Friar Laurence's cell be married.
Here is for thy pains.                              *(offers her some coins)*

NURSE:
No, truly sir–not a penny.

ROMEO:
Go to–I say you shall.

NURSE:                                              *(taking coins)*
This afternoon, sir? Well, she shall
be there.

## Act Two · Scene 4                                vernacular

ROMEO:
And you wait, Nurse, behind the wall
of the abbey. Within an hour, my servant
will bring you ropes—tied up to make
a ladder—which I will use tonight.
Farewell!—my best to your mistress.

NURSE:
Yes, a thousand times. *[both exit]*

## Act Two · Scene 5 **scene description**

Juliet, having waited three hours for the Nurse
to return from her meeting with Romeo, is at her
wits' end. Finally the Nurse arrives and after playfully prolonging Juliet's pain, the Nurse tells her of
Romeo's plans.

## Act Two · Scene 5                                vernacular

JULIET:
It was nine o'clock when I sent the
nurse: she promised to return in half
an hour. It is now noon; and from nine
till twelve is three long hours,—yet
she hasn't come back. If she were in
love, and felt youthful passion, she
would move with the speed of a ball.
*[Nurse enters]* Oh God, she's here! Oh
sweet Nurse, tell me the news? Did you
meet with him?

NURSE:
I'm exhausted, give me a moment; ugh,
my bones ache!

JULIET:
I wish you had my bones, and I had your
news; come on, I beg you, speak;—
good, good Nurse, speak.

NURSE:
Jesus, what's the rush—can't you wait a bit?
Can't you see I'm out of breath?

JULIET:
How can you be out of breath, when you
have enough breath to say—you are
out of breath? Is your news good, or
bad? Answer that; is it good or bad?

NURSE:
Lord, my head aches! what a headache
I have! It pounds as though it would

## Act Two · Scene 4  **original abridged**

ROMEO:
And stay, good Nurse, behind the abbey
wall—within this hour my man shall
bring thee cords made like a tackled
stair, which must be my convoy in the
night. Farewell!—commend me to thy mistress.

NURSE:
Ay, a thousand times. *[both exit]*

## Act Two · Scene 5  **original abridged**

JULIET:
The clock struck nine, when I did send
the nurse: in half an hour she promised
to return. Now is the sun upon the high-
most hill; and from nine till twelve is
three long hours,—yet she is not come.
Had she affections, and warm youthful
blood, she'd be as swift in motion as a
ball. *[Nurse enters]* O God, she comes!
O honey Nurse, what news? Hast thou met
with him?

NURSE:
I am aweary, give me leave awhile; fie,
how my bones ache!

JULIET:
I would thou hadst my bones, and I thy
news; nay come, I pray thee, speak;—
good, good Nurse, speak.

NURSE:
Jesu, what haste—can you not stay awhile?
Do you not see that I am out of breath?

JULIET:
How are thou out of breath, when thou
hast breath to say—that thou art
out of breath? Is thy news good,
or bad? Answer to that; is't good or bad?

NURSE:
Lord, how my head aches! what a headache
have I? It beats as it would fall in

## Act Two · Scene 4  **stage directions**

*(Nur exits DL, Rom exits UR)*

## Act Two · Scene 5  **stage directions**

*(enters SL carrying stool which she sets LC, sits)*

*(Nur enters SL, Jul runs to her)*

*(Nur x to stool and sit)*

*(x to Nur)*

*(kneels L of Nur)*

---

**Act Two · Scene 5**          **vernacular**

---

break in twenty pieces. My back—*[Juliet starts to rub Nurse's back]* the other side,—oh, my back, my back!

JULIET:
Truly, I'm sorry that you're not well.
Sweet, sweet, sweet Nurse, tell me,
what did my love say?

NURSE:
Have you got permission to go to
confession today?

JULIET:
I have.

NURSE:
Then get on over to Friar Laurence's.
There awaits a husband who will make
you his wife. Get to the church. I must
fetch the ladder which your love will
climb when it is dark.

JULIET:
My trusty Nurse, farewell. *[they exit]*

---

**Act Two · Scene 6  scene description**

---

This brief scene takes place at Friar Laurence's cell where Romeo and the friar are awaiting Juliet's arrival. The friar is praying that this marriage will have no harmful consequences.

Romeo is waiting on pins and needles for Juliet to appear. She finally does and the friar, observing their passionate greeting, decides he must marry them quickly.

---

**Act Two · Scene 6**          **vernacular**

---

*[enter Friar Laurence and Romeo]*
FRIAR LAURENCE:
May heaven smile upon this holy act,
so that no regrets may haunt us
afterwards.

ROMEO:
Amen, amen! But come what may, nothing
could counteract the joy I feel from
every minute in her sight!

FRIAR LAURENCE:
Such extreme passion ends up in
extremity, therefore, love with
moderation. Here comes the lady.

## Act Two · Scene 5 **original abridged**

twenty pieces. My back—*[Juliet starts to rub Nurse's back]* t' other side,— O, my back, my back!

JULIET:
I' faith, I am sorry that thou art not well. Sweet, sweet, sweet Nurse, tell me, what says my love?

NURSE:
Have you got leave to go to shrift today?

JULIET:
I have.

NURSE:
Then hie you hence to Friar Laurence's cell. There stays a husband to make you a wife. Hie you to church. I must fetch a ladder, which your love must climb when it is dark.

JULIET:
Honest Nurse, farewell. *[they exit]*

## Act Two · Scene 6 **original abridged**

*[Romeo and Friar Laurence enter]*
FRIAR LAURENCE:
So smile the heavens upon this holy act, that after-hours with sorrow chide us not.

ROMEO:
Amen, amen! But come what sorrow can, it cannot countervail the joy that one short minute gives me in her sight!

FRIAR LAURENCE:
These violent delights have violent ends, therefore, love moderately. Here comes the lady.

## Act Two · Scene 5 **stage directions**

*(Jul rises, stands behind Nur, rubs her back)*

*(kisses Nur, runs off SL, Nur takes stool and follows, laughing)*

## Act Two · Scene 6 **stage directions**

*(enter SR xing towards DRC)*

*(Rom pacing DS of FrL)*

*(watching Rom)*

## Act Two · Scene 6 **vernacular**

JULIET: *[to Friar Laurence]*
Good evening.

ROMEO:
Ah, Juliet!

JULIET:
My love!

FRIAR LAURENCE:
Come, come with me, and we will be brief;
for, as you can see, I don't dare leave
you alone, till you are joined in holy
matrimony. *[they exit]*

## Act Three · Scene 1 **scene description**

It is the hottest part of the day and Benvolio
and Mercutio are in the town square. Benvolio,
aware that this is the time of day when tempers
could flare, advises Mercutio that they should go inside. Mercutio makes fun of Benvolio.

At that moment, Tybalt comes into the square
looking for Romeo. Mercutio tries to pick a fight
with him but Tybalt is intent on finding Romeo (remember Tybalt has sent a challenge to Romeo earlier that Romeo has had no time to respond to and
probably has not even seen).

Romeo appears at this moment and Tybalt publicly insults him. Romeo, not wishing to have a fight
with his new cousin-in-law, tries to brush off the insult. This apparent cowardice on the part of
Romeo, infuriates Mercutio and he challenges
Tybalt to fight.

Tybalt and Mercutio go at it and Romeo desperately tries to break them up. He steps between
them and in the confusion, Tybalt stabs Mercutio
and then runs off.

Mercutio, realizing that he has been mortally
wounded, curses both the Montagues and the
Capulets and, aided by Benvolio, staggers off to
die.

Romeo realizes that his refusal to accept the
challenge has resulted in Mercutio's death. He must
now avenge that death in order to regain his honor.

## Act Three · Scene 1 **vernacular**

*[enter Benvolio and Mercutio]*
BENVOLIO:
I beg you, good Mercutio, let's go home.
It's hot, the Capulets are out and about, and
if we run into them, there's bound to be a fight.

MERCUTIO: *[making fun of Benvolio's
seriousness]*
Come on, come on, you're as quick to
quarrel as anyone in Italy! and you
warn me about fighting?

BENVOLIO:
By heaven, here comes a Capulet.

MERCUTIO:
By hell, I don't care.

TYBALT:
Gentlemen, good afternoon; a word with
you.

MERCUTIO: *[looking for a fight]*
Only one word? Pair it with something
else; how 'bout a word and a blow?

TYBALT:
You'll find me very willing sir, given
the chance.

## Act Two · Scene 6   **original abridged**

JULIET: *[to Friar Laurence]*
Good even.

ROMEO:
Ah, Juliet!

JULIET:
My love!

FRIAR LAURENCE:
Come, come with me, and we will make short work; for, by your leaves, you shall not stay alone, till holy church incorporate two in one. *[they exit]*

## Act Two · Scene 6   **stage directions**

*(Jul enters SR x to FrL, curtsies to FrL)*

*(they meet and embrace DS of FrL)*

*(xing between them)*

*(escorts them off SR)*

## Act Three · Scene 1   **original**

*[enter Benvolio and Mercutio]*
BENVOLIO:
I pray thee, good Mercutio, let's retire. The day is hot, the Capulets abroad, and, if we meet, we shall not 'scape a brawl.

MERCUTIO: *[poking fun at Benvolio's seriousness]*
Come, come, thou art as hot a Jack in thy mood as any in Italy! And thou wilt tutor me from quarreling?

BENVOLIO:
By my head, here comes a Capulet.

MERCUTIO:
By my heel, I care not.

TYBALT:
Gentlemen, good den; a word with you.

MERCUTIO: *[looking for a fight]*
But one word? Couple it with something; make it a word and a blow.

TYBALT:
You shall find me apt enough to that, sir an you will give me occasion.

## Act Three · Scene 1   **stage directions**

*(enter UC, Mer has his sword out and he's practicing sword moves)*

*(x C lunging with sword)*

*(seeing Tyb DL, x to Mer, whisper to him)*

*(x to them)*

*(xing closer to Tyb)*

## Act Three · Scene 1 scene description

*Continued*

Tybalt returns and this affords Romeo the opportunity he seeks. They fight and Tybalt is slain. Benvolio reminds Romeo of the Prince's decree regarding fighting in the streets and urges Romeo to run, which he does.

The Prince, Capulet, Lady Capulet, Montague and Lady Montague all come on and the Prince asks Benvolio who began the fight. Benvolio promptly tells him what happened. Lady Capulet demands revenge on Romeo.

Montague points out that Mercutio and Romeo were friends and that Romeo merely took the law into his own hands when he killed Tybalt for killing Mercutio.

The Prince, taking all this into consideration, decides that Romeo should be exiled from Verona.

## Act Three · Scene 1   vernacular

MERCUTIO:
Don't you ever take a chance without it being given to you?

BENVOLIO: *[trying to quiet them both]*
We're in a public place: either go somewhere private, or else break it up; everyone's looking.

MERCUTIO:
Men's eyes were made to look; I will not budge!

TYBALT:
Well, let it be, sir! here comes the man I was looking for. Romeo, you are a villain.

ROMEO:
Tybalt, the reason I have to love you prevents me from accepting your challenge. I am not a villain, therefore farewell.

TYBALT:
Boy! You have insulted me; therefore turn, and draw your sword.

ROMEO:
I swear I never hurt you; but love you more than you know. Good Capulet,— whose name I love as dearly as my own, —don't be insulted.

MERCUTIO:
Oh, vile! Backing down? Tybalt! Ratcatcher!

TYBALT:
What do you want with me?

MERCUTIO:
King of cats, just one of your nine lives.

TYBALT:
I'm at your service!

Act Three · Scene 1 **stage directions**

MERCUTIO:
Could you not take some occasion without giving?

*(flicking his sword at Tyb)*

BENVOLIO: *[trying to quiet them both]*
We talk here in the public haunt of men: either withdraw into some private place, or else part; here all eyes gaze on us.

*(stepping between them)*

MERCUTIO:
Men's eyes were made to look; I will not budge!

TYBALT:
Well, peace be with you, sir! Here comes my man. Romeo, thou art a villain.

*(Rom enters UC, sees Ben & Mer, starts xing down, Tyb x to meet Rom C, Ben & Mer counter DL to watch, Mer puts his sword away)*

ROMEO:
Tybalt, the reason I have to love thee doth excuse the appertaining rage to such a greeting. Villain am I none, therefore farewell.

*(bows to Tyb, starts off towards UR)*

TYBALT:
Boy! Injuries thou hast done me; therefore turn, and draw.

ROMEO:
I do protest, I never injured thee; but love thee better than thou canst devise; good Capulet,—which name I tender as dearly as mine own,—be satisfied.

*(turning back to Tyb)*

*(starts off UR again)*

MERCUTIO:
O, vile submission!
Tybalt! You ratcatcher!

*(xing DS, places himself between Rom and Tyb and draws his sword on Tyb)*

TYBALT:
What would'st thou with me?

MERCUTIO:
King of cats, nothing but one of your nine lives.

TYBALT:
I am for you!

*(draws his sword and holds it up to Mer's in "ready" position)*

**Act Three·Scene 1** **vernacular**

ROMEO:
Noble Mercutio, put up your sword.

MERCUTIO: *[to Tybalt]*
Come, sir!

ROMEO:
Tybalt! Mercutio!—the prince has
forbidden...
Stop, Tybalt! Good Mercutio!
*[Tybalt stabs Mercutio and exits]*

MERCUTIO:
I am hurt.—A curse on both your houses!
—I am dying.

BENVOLIO:
What, are you hurt?

MERCUTIO:
Yes, yes, a scratch, a scratch. Oh my
god, it will do.

ROMEO:
Have courage, man; the cut can't have
been that bad.

MERCUTIO:
No, it's not as wide as a church-door;
but it's enough, it'll do—a curse
on both your houses!—Why the devil
did you try to part us? I was hurt under
your arm.

ROMEO:
I thought it was for the best.

MERCUTIO:
Help me into some house, Benvolio, or
I shall faint; a curse on both your
houses! They have made a corpse of me!
*[exit Benvolio and Mercutio]*

ROMEO:
My true friend was hurt on my account;
my reputation's ruined! Oh sweet Juliet,
your beauty has made me a coward.

| **Act Three·Scene 1 original abridged** | **Act Three·Scene 1    stage directions** |
|---|---|

ROMEO:
Gentle Mercutio, put thy rapier up.

*(stepping in towards Mer trying to stop them)*

MERCUTIO: *[to Tybalt]*
Come, sir!

*(tapping Tyb's blade with his, they start to fight\*)*

ROMEO:
Tybalt! Mercutio!—the prince hath
forbidden...
Hold, Tybalt! Good Mercutio!
*[Tybalt stabs Mercutio and exits]*

*(Ben ad libs\* as Rom steps between Tyb and Mer, as he does so, Tyb stabs Mer and runs off UC, Mer takes two steps DS, sinks to ground)*

MERCUTIO:
I am hurt.—A plague o' both the houses!—
I am sped.

BENVOLIO:
What, art thou hurt?

*(Rom and Ben x to either side of Mer)*

MERCUTIO:
Ay, ay, a scratch, a scratch. Marry, 'tis
enough.

ROMEO:
Courage, man; the hurt cannot be much.

MERCUTIO:
No, 'tis not so wide as a church-door;
but 'tis enough, twill serve—a plague
o' both your houses!—Why the devil came
you between us? I was hurt under your arm.

ROMEO:
I thought all for the best.

MERCUTIO:
Help me into some house, Benvolio, or
I shall faint; a plague o' both your
houses! They have made worm's meat of me!
*[exit Benvolio and Mercutio]*

*(Ben & Rom help Mer to stand, Ben takes Mer off SR)*

ROMEO:
My very friend hath got his mortal hurt in
my behalf; my reputation stained! O sweet
Juliet, thy beauty hath made me effeminate.

*(standing C, looking SR)*

**Act Three · Scene 1**                    **vernacular**

BENVOLIO: *[reentering]*
Oh Romeo, Romeo! brave Mercutio's dead!

ROMEO:
This is only the beginning of the end.

BENVOLIO:
Here comes angry Tybalt back again.
*[Tybalt reenters]*

ROMEO:
He's alive and triumphant! and Mercutio's
dead! Now, Tybalt, take back the
"villain" you called me; Mercutio's
soul is floating just above our heads,
either you, or I, or both of us, must
go with him. *[they fight, Tybalt is slain]*

BENVOLIO:
Romeo, run, get going! The Prince will
doom you to death if you are caught
—get lost!—be gone!—away!

ROMEO:
Oh! I am at the mercy of the fates!

BENVOLIO:
Why are you standing there? *[Romeo exits]*

*[enter Prince, Capulet, Lady Capulet
Montague, Lady Montague and servants]*

PRINCE:
Where are the villains who began this fray?

BENVOLIO:
Oh noble prince, I can tell you—there
lies the man, *[pointing to Tybalt]* who
was killed by young Romeo, and who killed
your cousin, brave Mercutio.

LADY CAPULET:
Tybalt, my cousin!—Oh, my brother's
child!—Prince, as you are true, for

| Act Three · Scene 1 **original abridged** | Act Three · Scene 1 **stage directions** |
|---|---|

BENVOLIO: *[reenters]*
O Romeo, Romeo! brave Mercutio's dead!

*(reenters SR, stands SR)*

ROMEO:
This but begins the woe, others must end.

BENVOLIO:
Here comes the furious Tybalt back again.
*[Tybalt reenters]*

*(Tybalt reenters UC)*

ROMEO:
Alive in triumph! and Mercutio slain? Now,
Tybalt, take the "villain" back again,
that late thou gavest me; Mercutio's soul
is but a little way above our heads,
either thou, or I, or both, must go with
him. *[they fight and Tybalt is slain]*

*(Rom pulls out his sword,
Tyb x DC to meet Rom, they
fight\*)*

*(Tyb falls C with his head
downstage)*

BENVOLIO:
Romeo, away, be gone! The Prince will doom
thee death if thou art taken—hence!—be
gone!—away!

*(x to Rom)*

ROMEO:
O! I am fortune's fool!

BENVOLIO:
Why dost thou stay? *[Romeo exits]*

*(Rom runs off SR)*

*[enter Prince, Capulet, Lady Capulet,
Montague, Lady Montague and Servants]*

*(Pr enters UC x to US of Tyb, Cap and LaC
enter DL, LaC x to Tyb, kneel, Cap stand
DLC, Mont & LaM enter UR x to Ben,
Balt & Ab enter UR and stand, Greg & Sam
enter DL and stand)*

PRINCE:
Where are the vile beginners of this fray?

BENVOLIO:
O noble prince, I can discover all: there
lies the man, *[pointing to Tybalt]* slain
by young Romeo, that slew thy kinsman,
brave Mercutio.

*(x DR of Pr)*

LADY CAPULET:
Tybalt, my cousin!—O my brother's
child!—Prince, as thou art true,

## Act Three · Scene 1 — vernacular

this blood of mine, shed blood of
Montague!

PRINCE:
Benvolio, who began this bloody fray?

BENVOLIO:
Tybalt!—who's dead, who Romeo killed.
Tybalt killed bold Mercutio and then
Tybalt ran off, but shortly he returned
to Romeo and they went at it like
lightning. Before I could part them,
Tybalt was slain. This is the truth.

LADY CAPULET:
He is a relative of the Montagues, his partiality
makes him lie, he's not speaking the truth. I beg
for justice, which you prince, must give;
Romeo killed Tybalt, Romeo must not live.

PRINCE:
Romeo killed him; he killed Mercutio.

MONTAGUE:
Romeo was Mercutio's friend; his offense
merely carried out what the law would
have done—put Tybalt to death.

PRINCE:
And for that offense, we exile him.
Let Romeo leave quickly, or else, if
he is found, he will be doomed to death.
*[all exit]*

## Act Three · Scene 2 scene description

Juliet is back in her room anxiously awaiting
nightfall and Romeo's arrival as has been previously
arranged. The Nurse enters, obviously distraught,
and tells Juliet that Romeo has killed Tybalt and that
Romeo has been banished.

Juliet curses Romeo, but when the Nurse
speaks ill of him, Juliet quickly turns on her and de-
fends Romeo, regretting her momentary betrayal of
him.

## Act Three · Scene 2 — vernacular

JULIET: *[enters]*
Move along quicker, you fiery sun; set
in the west, and bring on cloudy night.
Come night! come Romeo! come gentle
night; give me my Romeo.
*[seeing Nurse]*
Oh, here comes my Nurse. *[realizing Nurse
is very upset]* Now Nurse, what's the news?
Why are you wringing your hands?

## Act Three · Scene 1 **original abridged**

for blood of ours, shed blood of
Montague!

PRINCE:
Benvolio, who began this bloody fray?

BENVOLIO:
Tybalt!—here slain, whom Romeo's hand
did slay. Tybalt hit the life of stout
Mercutio and then Tybalt fled, but by and
by comes back to Romeo, and to't they go
like lightning. Ere I could part them,
was Tybalt slain. This is the truth.

LADY CAPULET:
He is a kinsman to the Montague, affection
makes him false, he speaks not true. I beg
for justice, which thou prince, must give;
Romeo slew Tybalt, Romeo must not live.

PRINCE:
Romeo slew him; he slew Mercutio.

MONTAGUE:
Romeo was Mercutio's friend; his fault
concludes but, what the law should end,
the life of Tybalt.

PRINCE:
And for that offense, immediately we do
exile him hence. Let Romeo hence in haste,
else when he is found, that hour is his last.
*[all exit]*

## Act Three · Scene 2 **original abridged**

JULIET: *[enters]*
Gallop apace, you fiery-footed steeds,
towards Phoebus' lodging, and bring in
cloudy night. Come, night! come, Romeo!
come gentle night; give me my Romeo.
*[seeing Nurse]*
O, here comes my nurse. *[realizing
Nurse is distraught]* Now Nurse, what
news? Why dost thou wring thy hands?

## Act Three · Scene 1 **stage directions**

*(still kneeling)*

*(x with LaM to DR of Ben)*

*(Pr exits UC, as Cap nods to Greg & Sam
who carry Tyb off DL, LaC follows,
as Ab & Balt exit UR, Cap, Mont & LaM
stare at each other for a moment, then
Cap exits DL as Mont & LaM & Ben exit UR)*

## Act Three · Scene 2 **stage directions**

*(Jul enters SL with stool
which she sets LC, kneels
atop stool)*

*(Nur enters SL holding rope)*

*(Jul x to Nur)*

## Act Three • Scene 2 **scene description**

*Continued*

It is then that the full impact of the Prince's decree of banishment hits Juliet. Her overwhelming distress prompts the Nurse to take pity on her and she tells Juliet that she will find Romeo and bring him to her so that he may comfort her.

## Act Three • Scene 2    **vernacular**

NURSE: *[weeping]*
Ah, he's dead. He's dead! What a day!
He's gone, he's killed. He's dead!

JULIET:
Is Romeo slain?

NURSE:
I saw the wound.

JULIET:
Oh, my heart, break! Break at once!

NURSE:
Oh, Tybalt, Tybalt, that I should live
to see you dead!

JULIET:
Is Romeo slaughtered and is Tybalt dead?

NURSE:
Tybalt is gone and Romeo banished. Romeo,
who killed him, is banished.

JULIET:
Oh, god! Did Romeo kill Tybalt?

NURSE:
He did. He did! What a day, he did!

JULIET:
Oh, the heart of a snake, hidden behind
such a beautiful face. Oh that such
evil could be concealed in so gorgeous
a body.

NURSE:
There's no trust, no truth, no honesty
in men. This sorrow makes me feel old.
Shame on Romeo!

JULIET:
He was not meant to be shamed. Shame
would be ashamed in his presence.

| Act Three • Scene 2 **original abridged** | Act Three • Scene 2 **stage directions** |
| --- | --- |

NURSE: *[weeping]*
Ah, he's dead, he's dead! Alack the day!
He's gone, he's killed, he's dead!

*(Nur standing, numb)*

JULIET:
Romeo slain?

NURSE:
I saw the wound.

JULIET:
O break, my heart! Break at once!

*(falling to her knees)*

NURSE:
O Tybalt, Tybalt, that I should live to
see thee dead!

*(xing US of Jul to stool
and sitting)*

JULIET:
Is Romeo slaughtered and is Tybalt dead?

NURSE:
Tybalt is gone, and Romeo banished. Romeo,
that killed him, he is banished.

JULIET:
O God! Did Romeo's hand shed Tybalt's
blood?

NURSE:
It did, it did! Alas the day, it did!

JULIET:
O serpent heart, hid with a flowering
face! Oh, that deceit should dwell in
such a gorgeous palace.

NURSE:
There's no trust, no faith, no honesty
in men. These sorrows make me old. Shame
come to Romeo!

JULIET:
He was not born to shame. Upon his brow
shame is ashamed to sit.

*(stands, x to Nur)*

### Act Three · Scene 2 — vernacular

NURSE:
Will you speak well of the man who killed
your cousin?

JULIET:
Should I speak ill of the man who is
my husband? Oh, my poor lord, who shall
uphold your honor, when I, your new
bride have questioned it?—But why
did you kill my cousin? That cousin
would have killed my husband: my husband
is alive, this should cheer me; why
am I weeping then? Something else was
said, worser than Tybalt's death, that
murders me: "Tybalt is dead, and Romeo
—banished"—that—"banished", that
one word—"banished",—"Romeo is
banished!" There is no end, no limit,
measuring, boundaries, in that word's
consequences. Come Nurse, I will go
to my wedding bed; and let death, not
Romeo, take my maidenhead!

NURSE: *[comforting Juliet]*
Go to your room. I'll find Romeo and
bring him there to comfort you. I know
where he is. Listen to me, your Romeo
will be here tonight; I'll go to him;
he's hiding at Laurence's cell.

JULIET:
Oh, find him! And ask him to come and
take his last farewell. *[both exit]*

### Act Three · Scene 3 scene description

This scene takes place at Friar Laurence's where Romeo has gone to hide after killing Tybalt. Friar Laurence is just returning, having obviously gone out to discover what he can about the Prince's reaction to the fighting in the streets.

Friar Laurence tells Romeo that the Prince has not doomed him to death as would have been expected under the circumstances, but has instead exiled him. Romeo's response is that death would

### Act Three · Scene 3 — vernacular

*[enter Friar Laurence]*
FRIAR LAURENCE:
Romeo, come out.

ROMEO: *[enters]*
Father, what's the news?

FRIAR LAURENCE:
I bring you the news of the prince's
doom.

## Act Three · Scene 2 **original abridged**

## Act Three · Scene 2    **stage directions**

NURSE:
Will you speak well of him that killed
your cousin?

JULIET:
Shall I speak ill of him that is my
husband? Ah, poor my lord, what tongue
shall smooth thy name, when I, thy three-
hours' wife, have mangled it?—But
wherefore didst thou kill my cousin?
That cousin would have killed my husband:
my husband lives; this is comfort;
wherefore weep I then? Some word there
was, worser than Tybalt's death, that
murdered me: "Tybalt is dead, and Romeo—
banished"—that—"banished", that one
word—"banished",—"Romeo is banished!"
There is no end, no limit, measure, bound
in that word's death. Come, Nurse—I'll to
my wedding bed; and death, not Romeo,
take my maidenhead!

*(xing DL, in her own world)*

*(sinking to her knees)*

NURSE: *[comforting Juliet]*
Hie to your chamber. I'll find Romeo to
comfort you. I wot well where he is. Hark
ye, your Romeo will be here at night;
I'll to him; he is hid at Laurence's cell.

*(rise x to US of Jul and
comfort her)*

*(helping Jul rise)*

JULIET:
O, find him! And bid him come to take his
last farewell. *[both exit]*

*(walking off SL with Nur)*

## Act Three · Scene 3 **original abridged**

## Act Three · Scene 3    **stage directions**

*[enter Friar Laurence]*
FRIAR LAURENCE:
Romeo, come forth.

*(Greg enters UL, takes stool
off UL as FrL enters SR
calling to UR)*

ROMEO: *[enters]*
Father, what news?

*(enters from UR, x to L of
FrL who is RC)*

FRIAR LAURENCE:
I bring thee tidings of the prince's
doom.

## Act Three · Scene 3 scene description

*Continued*

have been easier to deal with because he cannot stand the idea of being sent away from the town where Juliet lives.

The Friar tries to reason with Romeo but he is inconsolable and insists that the Friar cannot understand his pain because he has not experienced what Romeo is going through.

At that moment, there is a knock at the door and the Friar tries to get Romeo to go back and hide which Romeo refuses to do.

Fortunately, it is only the Nurse who is arriving from Juliet. She notes that Romeo and Juliet are behaving in the same "weeping and blubbering" manner and she tells Romeo to stand up and act like a man.

The Friar picks up the Nurse's cue—he too has had enough of this moaning and groaning—and he tells Romeo that he should thank his lucky stars that he has Juliet for his love; that he won the duel with Tybalt and was not himself killed; and that he was not condemned to death—merely banished.

The Friar then tells Romeo to go to Juliet and to comfort her and to leave before daybreak for Mantua where he must spend his exile till a pardon can be gotten from the Prince.

Romeo agrees to follow the Friar's advice.

## Act Three · Scene 3 vernacular

ROMEO:
What less than dooms-day is the prince's doom?

FRIAR LAURENCE:
A milder sentence came from his lips, not your death, but your banishment.

ROMEO:
Ah! banishment? have mercy, say death: for exile is more terrible than death: do not say—banishment.

FRIAR LAURENCE:
You are banished from Verona: be patient, this is merciful, and you can't see it.

ROMEO:
It is torture and not mercy—heaven is here, where Juliet lives. Every cat, and dog, and little mouse, every unworthy thing may see her, but Romeo may not —he is banished!

FRIAR LAURENCE:
Listen to me for just a moment.

ROMEO:
Oh, you will speak of banishment again.

FRIAR LAURENCE:
I'll give you strength to comfort you; misfortune's silver-lining, philosophy.

ROMEO:
Hang philosophy! Unless philosophy can make a Juliet.

FRIAR LAURENCE:
Let me reason with you about your situation.

ROMEO:
You can't talk about what you don't know. If you were as young as I am, Juliet your love, married for just one hour, Tybalt murdered, as mad about

| Act Three·Scene 3 **original abridged** | Act Three·Scene 3 **stage directions** |
|---|---|

ROMEO:
What less than dooms-day is the prince's
doom?

FRIAR LAURENCE:
A gentler judgment vanished from his lips,
not body's death, but body's banishment.

ROMEO:                                                   *(backing away from FrL*
Ha! banishment? be merciful, say death:       *towards C)*
for exile hath more terror than death:
do not say—banishment.

FRIAR LAURENCE:
From Verona art thou banished: be patient,
this is mercy, and thou seest it not.

ROMEO:
'Tis torture, and not mercy: heaven is
here, where Juliet lives. Every cat, and
dog, and little mouse, every unworthy
thing may look on her, but Romeo may not—
he is banished!

FRIAR LAURENCE:                                      *(FrL x to Rom)*
Hear me a little speak.

ROMEO:                                                   *(Rom x DC)*
O, thou wilt speak again of banishment.

FRIAR LAURENCE:
I'll give thee armour to comfort thee;
adversity's sweet milk, philosophy.

ROMEO:                                                   *(Rom sinks to his knees,*
Hang up philosophy! Unless philosophy       *facing DS)*
can make a Juliet.

FRIAR LAURENCE:                                      *(xing to Rom a little)*
Let me dispute with thee of thy
estate.

ROMEO:                                                   *(still facing DS)*
Thou canst not speak of that thou dost
not feel. Wert thou as young as I, Juliet
thy love, an hour married, Tybalt murdered,
doting like me and like me—banished,

her as I and like me—banished, then
you might speak, then you might tear
your hair, and fall to the ground, as
I do now. *[there is knocking]*

FRIAR LAURENCE:
Get up, someone's here; good Romeo,
hide. *[more knocking]* Hello, who's
there?—Romeo, get up; you will be
arrested—*[more knocking]* just a minute—
*[to Romeo]* stand up! *[more knocking]*
I'm coming, I'm coming—who's knocking
so hard! *[sees Nurse]* What do you want?

NURSE:
I come from Lady Juliet.

FRIAR LAURENCE:
Welcome then.

NURSE:
Oh holy friar, where's Romeo?

FRIAR LAURENCE:
There, wallowing in his own tears.

NURSE:
Oh, just like my mistress, just like
her! Like that she is, blubbering and
weeping, weeping and blubbering!—Stand
up, stand up, stand if you are a man:
for Juliet's sake, for her sake, rise
and stand!

FRIAR LAURENCE:
Get up, man! Your Juliet is alive,
in that you are fortunate: Tybalt would
have killed you, but you killed Tybalt;
in that you are fortunate: the law,
that should have sentenced you to death,
became your ally, and turned that
sentence into exile; in that you are
fortunate: a pack of blessings have
landed on you; fortune smiles on you
with her finest gifts; but, like a
naughty, sulking little girl, you pout
about your good fortunes. Take care!

| **Act Three · Scene 3 original abridged** | **Act Three · Scene 3  stage directions** |
|---|---|
| then might'st thou speak, then might'st thou tear thy hair, and fall upon the ground, as I do now. *[there is knocking]* | *(Nur stamps\* on floor at SR entrance)* |
| FRIAR LAURENCE:<br>Arise, one knocks; good Romeo, hide thyself. *[more knocking]* Hark, who's there?—Romeo, arise; thou wilt be taken—*[more knocking]* stay awhile—*[to Romeo]* stand up! *[more knocking]* I come, I come—who knocks so hard! *[sees Nurse]* What's your will? | *(during this speech, FrL moves back and forth between SR entrance and Rom)*<br><br><br><br>*(at SR entrance)* |
| NURSE:<br>I come from Lady Juliet. | *(at SR entrance)* |
| FRIAR LAURENCE:<br>Welcome then. | *(relieved, FrL starts to usher Nur in)* |
| NURSE:<br>O holy friar, where's Romeo? | |
| FRIAR LAURENCE:<br>There, with his own tears made drunk. | *(indicating Rom)* |
| NURSE:<br>O, he is even in my mistress' case, just in her case! Even so lies she, blubbering and weeping, weeping and blubbering!—Stand up, stand up, stand an you be a man: for Juliet's sake, for her sake, rise and stand! | *(xing halfway to Rom)*<br><br><br>*(xing R of Rom)* |
| FRIAR LAURENCE:<br>Rouse thee, man! Thy Juliet is alive, there art thou happy: Tybalt would kill thee, but thou slew'st Tybalt; there are thou happy too: the law, that threatened death, became thy friend, and turned it to exile; there art thou happy: a pack of blessings light upon thy back; happiness courts thee in her best array; but, like a misbehaved and sullen wench, thou pout'st upon thy fortune and thy love. Take heed, take heed! Go, get thee to thy love, as was decreed, ascend her | *(xing L of Rom)*<br><br><br><br><br><br><br><br><br>*(kneels to Rom, comforting him)* |

**Act Three • Scene 3**                **vernacular**

Take care! Go, go to your love as was planned—climb up into her room and comfort her; but you must not stay till the break of day, because then you could not leave for Mantua; where you shall live till we can find a way to make your marriage known, reconcile your friends, get a pardon from the prince, and bring you back with twenty hundred thousand times more joy than you left with. *[to Nurse]* Go ahead, Nurse—send your lady my best; tell her to get everyone to bed. Romeo is coming.

NURSE:
Oh Lord, I could have stood here all night, to hear you speak: Oh, what a thing learning is!—My lord, I'll tell my lady you are coming. *[she exits]*

ROMEO:
I am revived by your good advice!

FRIAR LAURENCE:
Go ahead—good night. Spend some time in Mantua. I'll get word to your servant and he shall report to you from time to time what the news is here. Give me your hand, it's late. Farewell.

ROMEO:
Farewell. *[they exit]*

**Act Three • Scene 4 scene description**

This scene between Capulet, Lady Capulet and Paris takes place in the Capulet house. It is very late the same day and Paris, who has probably come to offer his condolences for Tybalt's death is leaving.

Capulet tells Paris that because of the death in the family, they haven't had the opportunity to speak further with Juliet about Paris' proposal. They know Juliet is miserable and—knowing nothing of her relationship with Romeo—they assume it is due to Tybalt's death.

**Act Three • Scene 4**                **vernacular**

*[enter Capulet, Lady Capulet and Paris]*
CAPULET:
Things have turned out so badly that I haven't had time to speak to my daughter. She loved her cousin Tybalt very much, and so did I;—well, we were born to die. It's very late—she won't come down tonight.

## Act Three·Scene 3 **original abridged**

chamber hence and comfort her; but look
thou stay not till the break of day, for
then thou canst not pass to Mantua; where
thou shalt live, till we can find a time
to blaze your marriage, reconcile your
friends, beg pardon of the prince, and
call thee back with twenty hundred
thousand times more joy than thou went'st
forth. *[to Nurse]* Go before, Nurse:
commend me to thy lady; and bid her hasten
all the house to bed. Romeo is coming.

NURSE:
Oh Lord, I could have stay'd here all the
night, to hear good counsel: O, what
learning is!—My lord, I'll tell my
lady you will come. *[Nurse exits]*

ROMEO:
How well my comfort is revived by this!

FRIAR LAURENCE:
Go hence: good night. Sojourn in Mantua.
I'll find out your man, and he shall
signify from time to time every good
hap to you, that chances here. Give me
your hand, 'tis late. Farewell.

ROMEO:
Farewell. *[they exit]*

## Act Three·Scene 4 **original abridged**

*[enter Capulet, Lady Capulet and Paris]*
CAPULET:
Things have fallen out sir, so unluckily
that we have had no time to move our
daughter. She loved her kinsman Tybalt
dearly, and so did I;—well, we were
born to die. 'Tis very late; she'll not
come down tonight.

## Act Three·Scene 3  **stage directions**

*(FrL rises and helps Rom up)*

*(exit SR)*

*(facing FrL)*

*(escorting Rom, they walk SR)*

*(shake hands)*

*(they exit SR)*

## Act Three·Scene 4  **stage directions**

*(Cap and Par enter DL with
LaC following, they x DLC
end up with Cap between
and slightly US of Par
and LaC)*

## Act Three · Scene 4 scene description

*Continued*

Capulet impulsively decides to consent to a marriage between Juliet and Paris, hoping that this might bring his daughter out of her deep depression.

They decide that the ceremony will take place on Thursday morning and Capulet sends Lady Capulet to inform Juliet of this news.

## Act Three · Scene 4   vernacular

PARIS:
This time of mourning is no time to woo. Madam, goodnight; my best to your daughter.

LADY CAPULET:
I'll tell her, and speak to her first thing in the morning; tonight she's shut up with her sorrow.

CAPULET:
Sir Paris, my child I think will be guided by me. Wife, go to her and tell her of Paris' love and tell her that next Wednesday—but wait! What is today?

PARIS:
Monday, my lord.

CAPULET:
Monday! ha, ha! Well, Wednesday is too soon. Thursday then;—on Thursday tell her she shall be married to this noble earl. *[to Paris]* Will you be ready?

PARIS:
My lord, I wish Thursday were tomorrow.

CAPULET:
Well get going—Thursday then. *[to Lady Capulet]* Go to Juliet before you go to bed; tell her wife, about this wedding day. *[to Paris]* Farewell, my lord, goodnight. *[they exit]*

## Act Three · Scene 5 scene description

It is almost daybreak and Romeo and Juliet have spent the night together in Juliet's room. It is now time for Romeo to depart for Mantua. This is naturally a very painful parting for them and they delay it as long as they can.

The Nurse then comes to tell them that Lady Capulet is approaching and, after promising to stay in touch as often as possible, Romeo departs.

## Act Three · Scene 5   vernacular

*[enter Romeo and Juliet]*
JULIET:
Must you go?

ROMEO:
Look, love, the stars are gone, and the dawn is coming, I must be gone and live, or stay and die.

## Act Three · Scene 4 **original abridged**

PARIS:
These times of woe, afford no times to
woo. Madam, goodnight; commend me to
your daughter.

LADY CAPULET:
I will, and know her mind early tomorrow;
tonight she's mewed up to her heaviness.

CAPULET:
Sir Paris, my child, I think will be ruled
by me. Wife, go you to her, acquaint her
of Paris' love; and bid her on Wednesday
next—but soft—what day is this?

PARIS:
Monday, my lord.

CAPULET:
Monday? ha, ha! Well, Wednesday is too
soon. Thursday let it be;—a Thursday,
tell her she shall be married to this
noble earl. *[to Paris]* Will you be ready?

PARIS:
My lord, I would that Thursday were
tomorrow.

CAPULET:
Well, get you gone—a Thursday be it
then. *[to his wife]* Go you to Juliet ere
you go to bed; prepare her, wife against
this wedding day. Farewell, my lord,
goodnight. *[they all exit]*

## Act Three · Scene 5 **original abridged**

*[enter Romeo and Juliet]*
JULIET:
Wilt thou be gone?

ROMEO:
Look, love, night's candles are burnt out,
and day stands tiptoe on the mountain tops;
I must be gone and live, or stay and die.

## Act Three · Scene 4 **stage directions**

*(kissing LaC's hand)*

*(as Par turns as if to exit
UC, Cap stops him with
his line)*

*(turning to LaC)*

*(Par exit UC, Cap and LaC
exit DL)*

## Act Three · Scene 5 **stage directions**

*(Sam & Greg enter from UL
with ladder, set it on
diagonal, exit UL, Rom
& Jul enter SL, arm in arm,
Rom ascends DS of ladder,
Jul ascends US, in silence)*

## Act Three · Scene 5 **scene description**

*Continued*

Lady Capulet arrives, and thinking that the tears she sees in Juliet's eyes are from mourning over Tybalt's death, tells Juliet that she must cease her grieving. She then goes on to tell her that Capulet, in order to cheer her up, has planned to have her married to Count Paris.

Juliet is naturally outraged by this news and says so. Just then Capulet comes in and when he hears Juliet's response, he is furious.

Juliet tries to plead with him but he won't listen and he tells her that if she refuses to marry Paris, she will be thrown out of his home and can starve in the streets for all he cares. Her parents storm out of her room leaving her with the Nurse.

When Juliet asks the Nurse for advice, the Nurse, very practically tells her that she should marry the count because as things stand, her marriage to Romeo is as good as useless.

Juliet thanks her for her advice and sends the Nurse to tell her parents that she will go to Friar Laurence to confess her sin of disobedience to her parents.

Once the Nurse is gone, Juliet reveals that she is furious with her and that she is really going to the Friar's for his advice about her situation.

## Act Three · Scene 5    **vernacular**

JULIET:
That light is not daylight, I know it.
So stay; you needn't leave yet.

ROMEO:
Let them take me. Let them put me to death. I'm willing, if you want it that way. Come death, and welcome! Juliet will have it so. It is not day!

JULIET:
It is, it is! Go, go on, away! *[they kiss]* Oh, now go on! Lighter and lighter it grows.

ROMEO:
Lighter and lighter it grows!—darker and darker our woes.

NURSE: *[enters]*
Madam!

JULIET:
What is it, Nurse?

NURSE:
Your mother is coming to your room.

ROMEO:
Farewell, farewell! One kiss, and I'll go.

JULIET:
Are you gone? You must write me every day.

ROMEO:
Farewell! I'll write you as often as I can.

JULIET:
Oh, do you think we shall ever meet again?

| Act Three·Scene 5 **original abridged** | Act Three·Scene 5    **stage directions** |
|---|---|
| JULIET:<br>Yon light is not daylight, I know it.<br>Therefore stay yet, thou need'st not to<br>be gone. | |
| ROMEO:<br>Let me be ta'en, let me be put to death,<br>I am content, so thou wilt have it so.<br>Come, death, and welcome! Juliet wills it<br>so. It is not day. | |
| JULIET:<br>It is, it is! Hence, be gone, away! *[they<br>kiss]* O, now be gone! More light and<br>light it grows. | *(kissing across the top<br>of the ladder)* |
| ROMEO:<br>More light and light!—more dark and<br>dark our woes! | |
| NURSE:*[enters]*<br>Madam. | *(poking her head in at SL<br>entrance)* |
| JULIET:<br>Nurse? | |
| NURSE:<br>Your lady mother's coming to your<br>chamber. | *(leaving them alone)* |
| ROMEO:<br>Farewell, farewell! One kiss, and I'll<br>descend. | *(they kiss again, Rom<br>descends)* |
| JULIET:<br>Art thou gone so? I must hear from thee<br>every day. | |
| ROMEO:<br>Farewell! I will omit no opportunity,<br>that may convey my greetings, love, to<br>thee. | *(from foot of ladder, looking<br>up to Jul)* |
| JULIET:<br>O, think'st thou we shall ever meet again? | |

**Act Three · Scene 5**        **vernacular**

ROMEO:
I know we will; and laugh at all this
in time to come.

JULIET:
Oh god!

ROMEO:
Adieu, adieu! *[Romeo exits]*

LADY CAPULET: *[entering]*
Ah, daughter! Are you up?

JULIET:
My lady mother.

LADY CAPULET: *[seeing Juliet's tears]*
What, what is it, Juliet?

JULIET:
Madam, I don't feel well.

LADY CAPULET:
Still weeping for your cousin's death?
What, do you think your tears can bring
him back from his grave? Even if they
could, you couldn't make him live;
therefore stop.

JULIET:
Yet let me weep for such a painful loss.

LADY CAPULET:
Your weeping will let you feel your
pain, but not your friend, for whom
you weep.

JULIET:
Feeling the loss so very much, I can
do nothing but cry for my friend.

LADY CAPULET:
But now I'll tell you good news, girl.

JULIET:
I can use good news right now. What
is it?

ROMEO:
I doubt it not; and all these woes shall serve
for sweet discourses in our time to come.

JULIET:
O god!

ROMEO:
Adieu! adieu! *[exits]*

*(exits DR)*

LADY CAPULET: *[entering]*
Ho, daughter! Are you up?

*(enters SL xing in a little,
stands looking up at Jul,
Nur follows LaC, stands
at SL entrance)*

JULIET:
My lady mother.

*(Jul remains on ladder,
looking off DR, weeping)*

LADY CAPULET: *[seeing Juliet's tears]*
Why, how now, Juliet?

JULIET:
Madam, I am not well.

LADY CAPULET:
Evermore weeping for your cousin's death?
What, wilt thou wash him from his grave
with tears? An if thou could'st, thou
could'st not make him live; therefore,
have done.

JULIET:
Yet let me weep for such a feeling loss.

LADY CAPULET:
So shall you feel the loss, but not the
friend, which you weep for.

JULIET:
Feeling so the loss, I cannot choose but
ever weep the friend.

LADY CAPULET:
But now I'll tell thee joyful tidings,
girl.

*(xing DS a little)*

JULIET:
And joy comes well in such a needy time.
What are they?

*(Jul slowly descends ladder
and x to R of LaC)*

**Act Three · Scene 5        vernacular**

LADY CAPULET:
Well, well, you have a very caring
father; one, who, to cheer you in your
sadness, has devised a surprise, that
neither you nor I expected.

JULIET:
Madam, what is it?

LADY CAPULET:
Indeed, my child, early next Thursday
morning, the gallant, young and noble
count Paris, at Saint Peter's church,
shall make you a joyful bride.

JULIET:
Now, by Saint Peter's church, and by
Peter too, he shall not make me a joyful
bride! I am amazed at this rush; that
I should get married before the man,
that would be my husband, even courts
me. I beg you to tell my lord and father,
madam, that I will not marry yet!

LADY CAPULET:
Here comes your father; tell him so
yourself, and see how he takes it.

CAPULET:
Well, wife? Have you told her our
decision?

LADY CAPULET:
Yes, sir; but she'll have no part of it.

CAPULET:
Just a minute, let me understand this,
let me understand this, wife. What?
No part of it? Doesn't she thank us?
Isn't she proud? Doesn't she feel
fortunate?

JULIET:
Not proud...but thankful...proud I could
never be of what I hate; but thankful
even for hate, that is meant with love.

| Act Three·Scene **5 original abridged** | Act Three·Scene 5    **stage directions** |
|---|---|

**LADY CAPULET:**
Well, well, thou hast a careful father;
one, who, to put thee from thy heaviness,
hath sorted out a sudden day of joy, that
thou expect'st not, nor I looked not for.

**JULIET:**
Madam, what day is that?

**LADY CAPULET:**
Marry, my child, early next Thursday morn,
the gallant, young, and noble gentleman,
the county Paris, at Saint Peter's
church, shall make thee there a joyful
bride.

**JULIET:**
Now by Saint Peter's church, and Peter          *(x DC)*
too, he shall not make me there a joyful
bride! I wonder at this haste; that I
must wed ere he, that should be husband,
comes to woo. I pray you, tell my lord          *(turning back to LaC)*
and father, madam, I will not marry yet!

**LADY CAPULET:**                                *(Cap strides into R of LaC*
Here comes your father; tell him so             *from SL)*
yourself, and see how he will take it.

**CAPULET:**
How now, wife? Have you delivered to her
our decree?

**LADY CAPULET:**
Ay, sir; but she will none.

**CAPULET:**
Soft, take me with you, take me with
you, wife. How! Will she none? Doth
she not give us thanks? Is she not
proud? Doth she not count her bless'd?

**JULIET:**
Not proud...but thankful...proud can I
never be of what I hate; but thankful
even for hate, that is meant love.

**Act Three • Scene 5**     **vernacular**

CAPULET:
What! what, nonsense! Thank me no
thankings, nor proud me no prouds, but
get your fine little self together by
next Thursday to marry Paris at Saint
Peter's church, or I'll drag you there
by your hair.

JULIET:
Good father, I beg you, on my knees,
let me say one word.

CAPULET:
Hang you, disobedient wretch! I tell
you what—you go to church on Thursday
or don't ever look me in the face. Speak
not, reply not, do not answer me!

NURSE:
God in heaven!

CAPULET: *[to Nurse]*
Keep your mouth shut!

NURSE:
Can't I speak?

CAPULET:
Quiet, you babbling fool!

LADY CAPULET: *[to Capulet]*
You are too angry.

CAPULET:
Dear God! It makes me mad. To answer
—"I won't wed,—I can't love,—I'm
too young,—I beg your pardon"—If
you won't wed, I'll pardon you! Live
where you will—you shall not live
with me. Think about it; I'm not
kidding!—hang, beg, starve, die
in the streets,—I'll not be
made a liar. *[Capulet exits]*

JULIET:
Can no one see the depth of my grief?

| Act Three·Scene 5 **original abridged** | Act Three·Scene 5 **stage directions** |
|---|---|
| **CAPULET:**<br>How now! how now, chop-logic! Thank me no thankings, nor proud me no prouds, but fettle your fine joints 'gainst Thursday next to go with Paris to Saint Peter's church, or I will drag thee on a hurdle thither. | *(xing down to L of Jul)* |
| **JULIET:**<br>Good father, I beseech you on my knees, hear me with patience. | *(sinking to her knees)* |
| **CAPULET:**<br>Hang thee, disobedient wretch! I tell thee what—get thee to church a Thursday or never after look me in the face. Speak not, reply not, do not answer me! | *(throwing his arms up in rage, x US of Jul, pace, turn back, x to R of Jul)* |
| **NURSE:**<br>God in heaven! | *(xing in to R of LaC)* |
| **CAPULET:** *[to Nurse]*<br>Hold your tongue! | *(yelling back to Nur)* |
| **NURSE:**<br>May not one speak? | |
| **CAPULET:**<br>Peace, you mumbling fool! | |
| **LADY CAPULET:** *[to Capulet]*<br>You are too hot. | *(stepping in a bit to Cap)* |
| **CAPULET:**<br>God! It makes me mad. To answer—"I'll not wed,—I cannot love,—I am too young,—I pray you, pardon me"—An you will not wed, I'll pardon you! Graze where you will—you shall not house with me. Look to't, think on't; I do not use to jest!—hang, beg, starve, die in the streets,—I'll not be forsworn. *[he exits]* | *(pacing, US and DS)*<br><br><br><br><br><br><br><br>*(storms out SL)*<br>*(there is a brief silence before Jul speaks)* |
| **JULIET:**<br>Is there no pity that sees into the bottom of | |

**Act Three · Scene 5               vernacular**

Oh, sweet mother, don't send me away!
Delay this marriage for a month, a week!

LADY CAPULET:
Don't talk to me! I've had it with you.
*[she exits]*

JULIET:
Oh God!—That even the heavens should
be working against me!—Oh Nurse, how
shall I prevent this? What do you say?
Comfort me, Nurse.

NURSE:
Truly, here it is. I think it would
be best for you to marry the count.
Oh, he's a lovely gentleman! I think
this second husband is better than your
first; and even if he weren't, your
first one's dead; or as good as dead,
with you here, and him there.

JULIET:
Do you mean this with all your heart?

NURSE:
And with my soul too; else curse them
both.

JULIET:
Amen!

NURSE:
What?

JULIET:
Well, you have comforted me greatly.
Go inside and tell my mother I have
gone, having displeased my father, to
Friar Laurence's to make confession
and to be absolved.

NURSE:
Indeed I will, and this is very wise
of you. *[Nurse exits]*

## Act Three · Scene 5 **original abridged**

my grief? O, sweet mother, cast me not away!
Delay this marriage for a month, a week!

LADY CAPULET:
Talk not to me! I have done with thee.
*[she exits]*

JULIET:
O God! That heaven should practice
stratagems upon so soft a subject as
myself!—O Nurse, how shall this be
prevented? Comfort me, counsel me. What
say'st thou? Some comfort, Nurse.

NURSE:
Faith, here it is. I think it best you
married with the county. O, he's a lovely
gentleman! I think you are happy in this
second match, for it excels your first;
or if it did not, your first is dead; or
'twere as good he were, as living here,
and you no use of him.

JULIET:
Speak'st thou from thy heart?

NURSE:
And from my soul too; else beshrew them
both.

JULIET:
Amen!

NURSE:
What?

JULIET:
Well, thou hast comforted me marvelous
much. Go in; and tell my lady I am gone,
having displeased my father, to Laurence's
cell, to make confession and to be
absolved.

NURSE:
Marry, I will and this is wisely done.
*[Nurse exits]*

## Act Three · Scene 5    **stage directions**

*(x to LaC)*

*(exits SL)*

*(turning DS to say this)*

*(xing up to R of Nur)*

*(with arm around her shoulder,
Nur brings Jul DLC)*

*(turns to Nur)*

*(Nur exits SL)*

---

### Act Three • Scene 5 — vernacular

JULIET:
Go counselor! You are no longer in my heart. I'll go to the friar to find out his remedy. If all else fails, I'll kill myself! *[she exits]*

---

### Act Four • Scene 1 — scene description

It is Tuesday morning now and Paris is at Friar Laurence's cell to discuss his upcoming marriage to Juliet. The Friar, aware of the predicament this would put them all in, is trying to get as much information as he can from Paris.

Paris explains that, while he has not personally spoken to Juliet about the matter, Capulet is hoping to bring Juliet out of her depression with the marriage.

Juliet then appears. Paris leaves them, believing that Juliet has come to make confession to the Friar.

Once alone with the Friar, Juliet begs him for advice about how to prevent this second marriage and tells him that she is ready to kill herself if need be rather than betray Romeo by marrying Paris.

Once the Friar realizes the intensity of her convictions, he devises a plan to save her. He tells her to go home and agree to the marriage. He then gives her a potion that he says will cause her to appear dead for forty-two hours.

She is to drink the potion the night before the proposed wedding. When Paris comes to get her for the ceremony, she will be presumed dead and brought to the tomb where the Capulets are all buried.

In the meantime, the Friar will have informed Romeo by letter of this plan and Romeo and he will be at the tomb when Juliet awakes. Romeo will then take Juliet back to Mantua with him. Juliet agrees to the plan and departs.

---

### Act Four • Scene 1 — vernacular

*[enter Friar Laurence and Count Paris]*
FRIAR LAURENCE:
On Thursday, sir? That's very soon.

PARIS:
My new father-in-law wants it that way.

FRIAR LAURENCE:
You say you don't know what the lady herself thinks?

PARIS:
She weeps so much for Tybalt's death, that I've had little chance to talk of love. Her father wisely hastens our marriage hoping to stop her tears. So that's the reason for this speed.

FRIAR LAURENCE:
Look sir, here comes the lady.

*[enter Juliet]*
PARIS:
It's good to see you, my lady. Have you come to make confession to the father?

JULIET:
Are you free now, holy father, or shall I come to you at evening mass?

FRIAR LAURENCE:
I am free now. *[to Paris]* My lord, we must ask you to leave us alone.

**Act Three · Scene 5 original abridged**

JULIET:
Go, counselor! Thou and my bosom henceforth shall be twain. I'll to the friar
to know his remedy. If all else fails,
myself have power to die. *[she exits]*

**Act Three · Scene 5    stage directions**

*(Jul exits SL as Sam & Greg
enter UL, take ladder UL)*

**Act Four · Scene 1 original abridged**

*[enter Friar Laurence and County Paris]*
FRIAR LAURENCE:
On Thursday, sir? The time is very short.

PARIS:
My father Capulet will have it so.

FRIAR LAURENCE:
You say you know not the lady's mind.

PARIS:
Immoderately she weeps for Tybalt's death,
and therefore have I little talked of
love. Her father, in his wisdom, hastes
our marriage, to stop the inundation of
her tears. Now do you know the reason of
this haste.

FRIAR LAURENCE:
Look sir, here comes the lady.

*[enter Juliet]*
PARIS:
Happily met, my lady. Come you to make
confession to this father?

JULIET:
Are you at leisure, holy father now, or
shall I come to you at evening mass?

FRIAR LAURENCE:
My leisure serves me now. *[to Paris]* My
lord, we must entreat the time alone.

**Act Four · Scene 1    stage directions**

*(enter SR, in conversation,
x DRC, FrL to L of Par)*

*(sees Jul enter SR)*

*(Par x to Jul, bows)*

*(x down to FrL)*

**Act Four · Scene 1**  **vernacular**

PARIS:
Juliet, till Thursday. Till then, adieu.
*[he exits]*

JULIET:
Oh, come weep with me.

FRIAR LAURENCE:
Ah, Juliet, I already know your trouble;
I've heard you must, on Thursday, be
married to this count.

JULIET:
Tell me, friar, how I can prevent it.
If, with your wisdom you cannot help
me, then with this knife, I want to die.

FRIAR LAURENCE:
Wait, daughter, I see some hope. If,
rather than marry count Paris, you have
the strength of will to kill yourself;
then it is likely you would undertake
something similar to death to escape
from it.

JULIET:
Oh, tell me to leap from off the top
of any tower, rather than to marry Paris;
and I would do it without any fear or
doubt, in order to remain a pure wife
for my sweet love.

FRIAR LAURENCE:
Then go home, be cheerful, consent to
marry Paris. Wednesday is tomorrow;
tomorrow night, take this vial and drink
the liquid. Immediately, a coldness
and a drowsiness will run through all
your veins; no pulse, no warmth, no
breath, shall indicate that you are
alive. And in this disguise of death,
you shall remain forty-two hours, and
then awaken as though from a pleasant
sleep. Now, when the bridegroom comes
to wake you from your bed, there he'll
find you dead. You shall be carried

## Act Four · Scene 1  **original abridged**

PARIS:
Juliet, on Thursday. Till then, adieu.
*[he exits]*

JULIET:
O, come weep with me.

FRIAR LAURENCE:
Ah, Juliet, I already know thy grief;
I hear thou must on Thursday next be
married to this county.

JULIET:
Tell me, Friar, how I may prevent it. If,
in thy wisdom thou canst give no help,
with this knife, I long to die.

FRIAR LAURENCE:
Hold, daughter; I do spy a kind of hope.
If, rather than to marry county Paris,
thou hast the strength of will to slay
thyself; then it is likely thou wilt
undertake a thing like death to 'scape
from it.

JULIET:
O, bid me leap, rather than marry Paris,
from off the battlements of yonder tower;
and I will do it without fear or doubt,
to live an unstained wife to my sweet love.

FRIAR LAURENCE:
Then; go home, be merry, give consent to
marry Paris. Wednesday is tomorrow;
tomorrow night, look that thou lie alone,
take thou this vial, and this liquor
drink thou off. Presently, through all
thy veins shall run a cold and drowsy
humor; no pulse, no warmth, no breath,
shall testify thou livest. And in this
borrowed likeness of death thou shalt
continue two and forty hours, and then
awake as from a pleasant sleep. Now,
when the bridegroom comes to rouse thee
from thy bed, there art thou dead. Thou

## Act Four · Scene 1  **stage directions**

*(slight bow, exit SR)*

*(taking a step DL)*

*(x to her, hand on her
shoulder)*

*(turning to FrL)*

*(takes knife out of her
waistband)*

*(Jul puts knife away)*

*(as he speaks, FrL x DR,
gets vial, x back to R of
Jul)*

## Act Four · Scene 1   vernacular

to the tomb where all the Capulets are buried. In the meantime, I will write to Romeo and tell him of our plan; and he shall come here; and he and I will be there when you awaken, and that very night Romeo shall take you to Mantua. This shall solve your problem.

**JULIET:**
Give it to me!

**FRIAR LAURENCE:**
Go now, be firm in your resolve. I'll send a friar, speedily to Mantua, with my letter to your lord.

**JULIET:**
Love, give me strength! Farewell, dear father. *[they exit]*

## Act Four · Scene 2   scene description

Back at the Capulet home, the Nurse has told Juliet's parents about her visit to Friar Laurence and they hope that he will be able to straighten her out.

Juliet returns home and apologizes to her father for her disobedience. He is so delighted by her apparent change of heart that he decides the wedding should take place Wednesday morning instead of Thursday.

Lady Capulet protests saying that they will not be ready that soon but Capulet insists and sends Juliet off with the Nurse to prepare for the wedding.

## Act Four · Scene 2   vernacular

*[enter Capulet, Lady Capulet and Nurse]*
**CAPULET:**
What? Has my daughter gone to Friar Laurence?

**NURSE:**
Yes, truly.

**CAPULET:**
Well, perhaps he can do some good with her. *[Juliet enters]*

**NURSE:**
Look, she returns from confession with a cheerful look.

**CAPULET:**
Well, well, my headstrong girl; where have you been?

**JULIET:**
Where I have learned how to repent for the sin of disobedience. Pardon me,

## Act Four • Scene 1  **original abridged**

shalt be borne to that same vault where
all the kindred of the Capulets lie. In
the meantime, shall Romeo by my letters
know of our drift; and hither shall he
come; and he and I will watch thy waking,
and that very night, shall Romeo bear
thee hence to Mantua. This shall free
thee from this present shame.

JULIET:
Give me, give me!

FRIAR LAURENCE:
Get you gone, be strong in this resolve.
I'll send a friar with speed to Mantua,
with my letter to thy lord.

JULIET:
Love, give me strength! Farewell, dear
father. *[they exit]*

## Act Four • Scene 2  **original abridged**

*[enter Capulet, Lady Capulet and Nurse]*
CAPULET:
What, is my daughter gone to Friar
Laurence?

NURSE:
Ay, forsooth.

CAPULET:
Well, he may chance to do some good on
her. *[Juliet enters]*

NURSE:
See, where she comes from shrift with
merry look.

CAPULET:
How now, my headstrong; where have you
been?

JULIET:
Where I have learned me to repent the
sin of disobedient opposition. Pardon,

## Act Four • Scene 1  **stage directions**

*(reaching for vial)*

*(giving Jul vial, escorting
her SR)*

*(they exit SR)*

## Act Four • Scene 2  **stage directions**

*(enter SL, Cap strides to
C with Nur and LaC following
and stopping LC, Nur to
R of LaC)*

*(Jul enters UL, x DL of LaC)*

*(curtsying to Cap)*

## Act Four · Scene 2    vernacular

I beg you! From now on I shall listen
to you.

CAPULET:
Why, I'm happy to hear it. This is the
way things should be. *[to Lady Capulet]*
Send for the count; tell him this. I'll
have you married tomorrow morning.

JULIET:
Nurse, will you go with me to help me
pick out the things I'll need for
tomorrow?

LADY CAPULET: *[to Capulet]*
No, not till Thursday; that will be
soon enough.

CAPULET:
Go, Nurse, go with her; we'll go to
church tomorrow. *[exit Juliet and Nurse]*

LADY CAPULET:
We don't have everything that we need;
and it's now almost night.

CAPULET:
Tush! everything will be alright, wife.
You go to Juliet, help to pick out her
dress; I'll go to Paris, to get him
ready. I'm so happy. *[they exit]*

## Act Four · Scene 3    scene description

We are now in Juliet's room and having selected what she needs for the wedding, Juliet is
asking the Nurse to leave her for the night.

Lady Capulet comes in to see if she can be of
assistance but Juliet tells her that everything is
ready and she asks her mother to leave.

Alone in her room, Juliet has a moment of
panic during which she almost calls them back, but
realizes that she must be strong and carry out her
plan.

She drinks the potion and falls into the death-
like sleep.

## Act Four · Scene 3    vernacular

*[enter Juliet and Nurse]*
JULIET:
Yes, those clothes are the best; but,
gentle Nurse, I beg you, leave me alone
tonight.

LADY CAPULET: *[entering]*
Are you busy? Do you need my help?

JULIET:
No, madam; we have picked out the things

| Act Four · Scene 2 **original abridged** | Act Four · Scene 2 **stage directions** |
|---|---|

I beseech you! Henceforward I am ever
ruled by you.

CAPULET:
Why, I am glad on't. This is as't                *(x to Jul)*
should be. *[to Lady Capulet]* Send for          *(throwing this line over*
the county; go tell him of this. I'll             *his shoulder to LaC as he*
have this knot knit up tomorrow morning.          *hugs Jul)*

JULIET:
Nurse, will you go with me to help me
sort such needful ornaments as you think
fit to furnish me tomorrow?

LADY CAPULET: *[to Capulet]*
No, not till Thursday; there is time
enough.

CAPULET:
Go, nurse, go with her; we'll to church
tomorrow. *[exit Juliet and Nurse]*          *(exit SL)*

LADY CAPULET:
We shall be short in our provision; 'tis      *(LaC x DR to Cap)*
now near night.

CAPULET:
Tush! all things shall be well, wife.
Go thou to Juliet, help to deck up her;
I'll to Paris, to prepare up him. My
heart is wondrous light. *[they exit]*        *(exit SL)*

| Act Four · Scene 3 **original abridged** | Act Four · Scene 3 **stage directions** |
|---|---|

*[enter Juliet and Nurse]*                   *(enter UL x to C,*
JULIET:                                        *referring to offstage*
Ay, those attires are best;—but, gentle      *garments, Nur is R of Jul)*
nurse, I pray thee, leave me to myself
tonight.

LADY CAPULET: *[entering]*                    *(enter UL x to them)*
What, are you busy? Need you my help?

JULIET:
No, madam; we have culled such necessaries

## Act Four • Scene 3                    vernacular

that are needed for tomorrow. So, if
you don't mind, leave me alone for now.

LADY CAPULET:
Good night. Get to bed.

JULIET:
Farewell! *[Lady Capulet and Nurse exit]*
God only knows when we shall meet again.
I'll call them back to comfort me. Nurse!
*[stops herself]* what could she do here?
This dismal scene I will have to act
alone. Come, vial. Romeo,
I come! This I drink to you.
*[she drinks and falls]*

## Act Five • Scene 1    scene description

This scene takes place in Mantua. Balthasar has
come there to tell Romeo the news of Juliet's *death*.
Romeo immediately decides that he must go back
to Verona and join Juliet in death. He instructs
Balthasar to hire horses for the trip.

When Balthasar has gone, Romeo decides that
he must locate some poison and remembers an
apothecary shop nearby.

## Act Five • Scene 1                    vernacular

*[enter Romeo and his servant, Balthasar]*
ROMEO:
You have news from Verona? What is it,
Balthasar? Do you have letters from
the friar? How is my lady? How is Juliet?

BALTHASAR:
Her body sleeps and her immortal soul is
with the angels; I saw her laid out
in her family's tomb and immediately
came to tell you.

ROMEO:
Is it true? Hire some horses; I will
go there tonight.

BALTHASAR:
I beg you sir, be patient. You look
pale and wild, and that can only mean
trouble.

ROMEO:
Go now, and do what I asked. Have you
no letters at all from the friar?

BALTHASAR:
No, my good lord.

## Act Four · Scene 3  original abridged

as are behoveful for our state tomorrow.
So, please you, let me now be left alone.

LADY CAPULET:
Good night. Get thee to bed.

JULIET:
Farewell! *[Lady Capulet and Nurse exit]*
God knows when we shall meet again. I'll
call them back again to comfort me. Nurse!
*[stopping herself]* what should she do here?
My dismal scene I needs must act alone.
Come, vial. Romeo, I come!
This do I drink to thee. *[she
drinks and falls]*

## Act Four · Scene 3  stage directions

*(Nur and LaC exit UL)*

*(kneels LC , takes vial and toasts)*

*(drinks and sinks to ground)*

## Act Five · Scene 1  original abridged

*[enter Romeo and his servant, Balthasar]*
ROMEO:
News from Verona! How now, Balthasar?
Dost thou not bring me letters from the
Friar? How doth my lady? How fares my
Juliet?

BALTHASAR:
Her body sleeps, and her immortal part
with angels lives; I saw her laid in her
kindred's vault, and presently took post
to tell it you.

ROMEO:
Is it even so? Hire post horses; I will
hence tonight.

BALTHASAR:
I do beseech you sir, have patience.
Your looks are pale and wild, and do
import some misadventure.

ROMEO:
Leave me, and do the thing I bid thee do.
Hast thou no letters to me from the friar?

BALTHASAR:
No, my good lord.

## Act Five · Scene 1  stage directions

*(Rom and Balt enter DR and play this
scene in DR part of stage while the
following pantomime\* takes place: Nur
enters UL, sees Jul, reacts, rushes off SL, reenters
with Cap, LaC, Sam & Greg following,
X to body, react appropriately, Cap nods
to Sam & Greg who carry Jul off UL, Cap,
LaC & Nur follow, as FrL enters UC with
cloth which he lays on ground near C,
Sam and Greg carry Jul in UC, place her
on cloth with her head DS, as Cap, LaC,
Nur, & Par position themselves on sides of
body as do Sam & Greg, FrL stands US of
cloth, FrL crosses himself, all others cross
themselves, with FrL leading, they all
exit UC, FrL moves to UR position offstage,
all others move to UL position offstage
and wait—this action should all be timed to
end as, or soon after, Rom exits from this
scene DR)*

## Act Five • Scene 1      vernacular

ROMEO:
It doesn't matter; get going and hire
those horses; I'll be there soon.
*[Balthasar exits]* Well Juliet, I will
lie with you tonight. Let's see, how
shall I do it? I remember an apothecary
who lives close by, and if a man needed
poison, this wretched man would sell
it to him. *[he exits]*

## Act Five • Scene 2      scene description

The action now shifts back to Verona and Friar
Laurence's cell. Friar John arrives and tells Friar
Laurence that he was unable to deliver the letter
Friar Laurence had given him for Romeo, having
been subjected to a quarantine in a house where
there was an outbreak of the plague.

Friar Laurence realizes that he will have to go to
the Capulet tomb alone to get Juliet and decides to
keep her with him at the church till he can get
word to Romeo.

## Act Five • Scene 2      vernacular

*[enter Friar John to Friar Laurence's cell]*
FRIAR JOHN:
Holy brother, are you here?

FRIAR LAURENCE: *[entering]*
This sounds like Friar John. Welcome
back from Mantua; what did Romeo say?

FRIAR JOHN:
I wasn't able to get to Mantua. While
I was still here in town, visiting the
sick, the health workers, suspecting
the house I was in was infected with
the plague, sealed it up, and wouldn't
let me go.

FRIAR LAURENCE:
Who took my letter to Romeo?

FRIAR JOHN:
I couldn't send it,—here it is,—
nor even get a messenger to bring it
to you, they were so afraid of spreading
the infection.

FRIAR LAURENCE:
What bad luck! Then I must go to the
tomb alone; within three hours Juliet
will awaken. I'll write to Mantua again,
and keep her with me till Romeo comes.
*[they exit]*

**Act Five · Scene 1    original abridged**

ROMEO:
No matter; get thee gone and hire
horses; I'll be with thee straight.
*[Balthasar exits]* Well, Juliet, I will
lie with thee tonight. Let's see for
means. I do remember an apothecary,
hereabouts he dwells, an if a man did
need a poison, here lives a wretch would
sell it him. *[Romeo exits]*

**Act Five · Scene 2    original abridged**

*[enter Friar John to Friar Laurence's cell]*
FRIAR JOHN:
Holy brother, ho!

FRIAR LAURENCE: *[entering]*
This should be the voice of Friar John.
Welcome from Mantua; what says Romeo?

FRIAR JOHN:
My speed to Mantua was stayed. Here in
this city, visiting the sick, the
searchers of the town, suspecting that I
was in a house where the infectious
pestilence did reign, sealed up the doors,
and would not let me forth.

FRIAR LAURENCE:
Who bore my letter then, to Romeo?

FRIAR JOHN:
I could not send it,—here it is again,—
nor get a messenger to bring it to thee, so
fearful were they of infection.

FRIAR LAURENCE:
Unhappy fortune! Now must I to the
monument alone; within this three hours
will fair Juliet wake. I will write again
to Mantua, and keep her at my cell till
Romeo come. *[they exit]*

**Act Five · Scene 1    stage directions**

*(exit DR)*

*(exit DR)*

**Act Five · Scene 2    stage directions**

*(enter SR, calling to UR)*

*(enter UR xing down, they
greet RC)*

*(xing DRC with FrL as he
speaks)*

*(hands FrL letter)*

*(FrJ exits SR, FrL exits UR)*

We are at the Capulet tomb and Romeo and Balthasar have just arrived there. Romeo instructs Balthasar to deliver a letter which Romeo has written to his father. He then takes the torch that Balthasar has and tells him to leave. Balthasar, fearing Romeo's intentions decides to hide nearby.

Romeo then goes to the place where Juliet is laid to rest and, after embracing and kissing her, he proceeds to drink his poison and dies.

The Friar arrives just as Juliet is beginning to stir. She does not immediately notice Romeo and the Friar points out his body and, hearing a noise tells her to quickly come away with him.

Juliet refuses to leave and the Friar departs alone. Juliet then notes that Romeo has killed himself with poison and wishes he had left her some to die with. Hearing the watchmen approaching, Juliet takes Romeo's dagger and stabs herself in the heart and dies.

The watch, having seen the light from Romeo's torch, arrives and discovers the bodies of Romeo and Juliet. A man is sent to rouse the Capulets, the Montagues and the Prince. Meantime another of the watch brings in Balthasar and the Friar whom he has discovered nearby.

The Prince arrives and questions the watch. They tell him about the Friar and Balthasar. He then asks the Friar what he knows about the deaths and the Friar supplies him with the details. Balthasar then produces the letter that Romeo had asked him to give to his father. The Prince reads the letter which confirms what the Friar has already told him.

The prince then turns to the two distraught fathers and chastises them for their hatred that has brought about the deaths of their two beloved children. Capulet and Montague then take hands and, standing before the horrible consequences of their feuding, finally make peace. And as the gloomy morning arrives, all depart to grieve.

*[enter Romeo and Balthasar]*
ROMEO:
Take this letter; deliver it to my father early in the morning. Give me the light; and on your life I order you, no matter what you hear or see, stay away.

BALTHASAR:
I'll go sir, and not bother you.

ROMEO:
Live, prosper and farewell, good fellow.

BALTHASAR: *[aside]*
All the same, I'll hide here; I'm worried about him, and I don't know what he has in mind. *[he exits]*

ROMEO:
Oh my love! My wife! Death, which has taken your life, has not altered your beauty. Ah, dear Juliet, why are you still so lovely? Here, here I will remain. Oh, here will I rest forever. Eyes, look at her for the last time! Arms, hold her for the last time! and lips, seal this bargain of death with a last kiss! *[takes out vial of poison]* Here's to my love! *[drinks]* Oh, honest apothecary! Your drugs are quick. So, I kiss you and die.

FRIAR LAURENCE: *[entering]*
Saint Francis, help me! How many times tonight have I tripped over gravestones? *[seeing Romeo]* Romeo! Oh, how pale he is! Ah, what ill-fate is this. *[Juliet starts to awaken]* The lady wakes.

JULIET:
Oh, good friar! Where is my lord? I remember where I'm supposed to be, and here I am. Where is Romeo?

| Act Five · Scene 3   **original abridged** | Act Five · Scene 3   **stage directions** |
|---|---|

*[enter Romeo and Balthasar]*
ROMEO:
Take this letter; early in the morning
see thou deliver it to my father. Give me
the light; upon thy life I charge thee,
whate'er thou hearest or seest, stand all
aloof.

*(enter UC, Balt has a torch)*

*(hands Balt letter)*

*(takes torch from Balt)*

BALTHASAR:
I will be gone sir, and not trouble you.

ROMEO:
Live and be prosperous and farewell,
good fellow.

*(gives Balt money pouch,
x down to Jul)*

BALTHASAR: *[aside]*
For all this same, I'll hide me hereabout;
his looks I fear, and his intents I doubt.
*[he exits]*

*(exits UC, stands above
USL very quietly with his
back to the audience)*

ROMEO:
O, my love! my wife! Death, that hath
sucked thy breath, hath had no power yet
upon thy beauty. Ah, dear Juliet, why art
thou yet so fair? Here, here will I remain.
O, here will I set up my everlasting rest.
Eyes, look your last! Arms, take your last
embrace! And lips, seal with a righteous
kiss a bargain to death! *[takes out vial]*
Here's to my love! *[drinks]* O true
apothecary! Thy drugs are quick. Thus with
a kiss I die.

*(kneels L of Jul, placing
torch on ground)*

*(kisses Jul, sinks down to L of Jul)*

FRIAR LAURENCE: *[entering]*
Saint Francis be my speed! How oft
tonight have my old feet stumbled
at graves? *[seeing Romeo]*
Romeo! O, pale! Ah, what an
unkind hour is guilty of this. *[Juliet
starts to awaken]* The lady stirs.

*(as FrL crosses from UR to
UC entrance, he says this,
enters UC, sees Rom & Jul,
xing down to them and
then to R of Jul)*

JULIET:
O comfortable friar! Where is my lord?
I do remember well where I should be, and
there I am. Where is my Romeo?

*(Jul turning to FrL)*

**Act Five • Scene 3                 vernacular**

FRIAR LAURENCE:
Lady, come away from that nest of death,
come, come away. Your husband is there,
dead. *[hearing a noise]* Hurry, the watch
is coming. I don't dare stay any longer.
*[he exits]*

JULIET:
Go, you go away, but I will stay.
What's this? A cup, in my
true-love's hand? I see,
he has poisoned himself.
Ah, drunk all, and left no drop
to help me follow? I'll kiss your lips,
perhaps some poison is still on
them to make me die. *[kisses Romeo]* Your
lips are warm!

WATCHMAN 1:
Lead on! Where is it?

JULIET:
A noise? Then I'll be quick. Oh kind
dagger! This is  your new sheath;
rust there, and let me die.
*[she stabs herself and dies]*

WATCHMAN 2: *[leading on Watchmen 1&3]*
This is where I saw the light.

WATCHMAN 1:
What a terrible sight! Juliet, bleeding,
just now dead, who was buried here two
days ago. Go, tell the Prince, run to
the Capulets, wake up the Montagues.

WATCHMAN 3: *[entering with Balthasar
and Friar Laurence]*
Here's Romeo's man. We found him in
the churchyard.

WATCHMAN 1:
Hold him till the Prince gets here.

Act Five · Scene 3    **original abridged**

Act Five · Scene 3    **stage directions**

FRIAR LAURENCE:
Lady, come from that nest of death, come,
come away. Thy husband there lies dead.
*[hearing a noise]* Stay not to question,
for the watch is coming. Come, go, good
Juliet. I dare no longer stay. *[he exits]*

*(UR offstage noise\*, FrL stands,
reacting to noise, in a
panic, he exits UC, x to
Balt and stands with him)*

JULIET:
Go, get thee hence, for I will not away.
What's here? A cup, closed
in my true love's hand?
Poison, I see, hath been his timeless end.
Ah, drunk all, and left no friendly
drop to help me after? I will kiss thy
lips; haply some poison yet doth hang on
them to make me die. *[kisses Romeo]* Thy
lips are warm!

*(kneels to Rom, takes vial)*

WATCHMAN 1:
Lead! Which way?

*(we hear this line from
offstage UR corner)*

JULIET:
Yea noise? Then I'll be brief. O happy
dagger! This is thy sheath;
there rust, and let me die.
*[stabs herself and dies]*

*(takes dagger from Rom
waistband, stabs\* herself,
falls R of Rom)*

WATCHMAN 2: *[leading on Watchmen 1 & 3]*
This is the place where the torch doth burn.

*(Watch 1&2&3 x to UC
entrance on this line)*

WATCHMAN 1:
Pitiful sight! Juliet bleeding and newly
dead, who here hath lain this two days
buried. Go, tell the Prince, run to the
Capulets, raise up the Montagues.

*(Watch 1&2&3 enter UC,
see bodies)*

WATCHMAN 3: *[entering with Balthasar
and Friar Laurence]*
Here's Romeo's man. We found him in the
churchyard.

*(Watch 2&3 exit US xing
L ad-libbing\*, Watch 3
returns immediately with
Balt & FrL to UC)*

WATCHMAN 1:
Hold him in safety, till the Prince comes
hither.

*(has crossed to L of bodies,
looking at them)*

WATCHMAN 3:
And a friar, trembling, sighing and
weeping.

WATCHMAN 1:
Hold him too.

PRINCE:
What misfortune wakes me so early?

CAPULET:
What is it that everyone's shouting
about?

LADY CAPULET:
Everyone in the street is crying "Romeo",
and "Juliet".

PRINCE:
What's happened?

WATCHMAN 1:
Sovereign, here is Romeo, dead; and
Juliet, who was already dead, warm and
newly dead.

CAPULET:
Oh heaven! Oh wife! look how our daughter
is bleeding!

LADY CAPULET:
Oh my!

MONTAGUE:
Oh, didn't I teach you better, what
bad manners is it to go before your
father to your grave?

PRINCE: *[to the watchmen]*
Bring forward the people under suspicion.
Tell me immediately, what do you know
about this?

FRIAR LAURENCE:
I will be brief—Romeo was the husband
of Juliet, and she was Romeo's faithful

## Act Five · Scene 3    original abridged

WATCHMAN 3:
And here is a friar, that trembles, sighs,
and weeps.

WATCHMAN 1:
Stay the friar too.

PRINCE:
What misadventure calls our person
from our morning's rest?

CAPULET:
What should it be, that they so shriek
abroad?

LADY CAPULET:
The people in the street cry "Romeo",
some "Juliet".

PRINCE:
What fear is this?

WATCHMAN 1:
Sovereign, here lies Romeo dead; and
Juliet, dead before, warm and
new killed.

CAPULET:
O heaven! O wife! look how our daughter
bleeds!

LADY CAPULET:
O me!

MONTAGUE:
O thou untaught! what manners is in this,
to press before thy father to a grave?

PRINCE: *[to the watchmen]*
Bring forth the parties of suspicion. Say
at once what thou dost know in this.

FRIAR LAURENCE:
I will be brief—Romeo was husband to
Juliet and she, Romeo's faithful wife.

## Act Five · Scene 3    stage directions

*(Watch 3 takes Balt & FrL
URC)*

*(these next four lines are
spoken quickly, offstage
as they follow Watch 2
from USL to UC entrance)*

*(Pr enters UC xing to US
of cloth, Watch 1 counters
SL as Mont & LaM x L of
Rom and kneel, and Cap &
LaC x R of Jul and kneel,
Watch 2 remains L of UC)*

*(Watch 3 brings Balt & FrL
to R of Pr)*

wife. I married them. *[to Capulet]* You would have married her to count Paris —she came to me and begged me to find some way to prevent this second marriage. I gave her a sleeping potion; which worked as I had hoped. In the meantime, I wrote to Romeo telling him to come here. But the fellow who was to deliver my letter was delayed. I came here alone; but, when I arrived, Romeo was already dead. She wakes up and I begged her to leave, but she would not go with me, but—apparently—killed herself. All this is true.

PRINCE:
We've always known you to be a holy man. Where's Romeo's man! What can he add to this?

BALTHASAR:
I brought my master the news of Juliet's death; and then he promptly came here from Mantua. He asked me to deliver this letter to his father.

PRINCE:
Give me the letter, I will read it. *[he reads letter to himself]* This letter proves the friar's words true. Capulet! Montague!—see the consequences of your hate; that heaven has killed your joys through love! You are all punished.

CAPULET:
Oh Montague, give me your hand.

PRINCE:
A gloomy peace has come to us with this morning's light. Come now, and we will talk more of these sad things; for there never was a story of more woe than this of Juliet and her Romeo.

| Act Five·Scene 3  **original abridged** | Act Five·Scene 3  **stage directions** |
|---|---|

I married them. *[to Capulet]* You, would
have married her to county Paris. She
comes to me and bid me devise some means
to rid her from this second marriage.
Gave I her a sleeping potion; which so took
effect as I intended. Meantime, I writ to
Romeo, that he should hither come. But,
he which bore my letter, was staid. All
alone, came I; but, when I came, here
lay Romeo, dead. She wakes; and I
entreated her come forth, she would
not go with me, but—as it seems—did
violence on herself. All this I know.

*(indicating Cap)*

PRINCE:
We still have known thee for a holy man.
Romeo's man! What can he say in this?

*(noticing Balt)*

BALTHASAR:
I brought my master news of Juliet's
death; and then in post he came from
Mantua to this same place. This letter
he bade me give his father.

PRINCE:
Give me the letter, I will look on it.
*[he reads letter to himself]* This letter
doth make good the friar's words. Capulet!
Montague!—see, what a scourge is laid
upon your hate, that heaven finds means to
kill your joys with love! All are punished.

*(Balt hands letter to Pr)*

CAPULET:
O Montague, give me thy hand.

*(Cap & Mont rise, x to DS
of bodies, shake hands)*

PRINCE:
A glooming peace this morning with it brings.
Go hence, to have more talk of these sad
things; for never was a story of more woe
than this of Juliet and her Romeo.

*(all exit slowly, mournfully, UC,
leaving bodies in tomb)*

(We have selected our punctuation based on the First Folio, the Fisher Quarto, and Staunton's
"The Plays of Shakespeare" (1858–1861). We have taken some minor liberties with Shakespeare's
text to accommodate our abridged version and, for this, we apologize to purists, to scholars and,
most of all, to Shakespeare!)

# "To what end are all these words?"

## (a discussion of the language in Shakespeare's plays)

Having read the play, let's take a little time to look at Shakespeare's language—very different from the way we speak today!

Language evolves over the course of time. Foreign influences, developments in technology, new slang and altered usages of words all affect the way we communicate. What is perfectly clear in 1996, might be almost incomprehensible by the year 2396.

At the time that Shakespeare wrote, English was evolving at a particularly furious pace.

In 1066, England had been conquered by Frenchmen (Normans) who made French the official language of England. The upper classes spoke French, the lower classes spoke English (which was at that time a kind of German called Saxon) while all church business was conducted in Latin.

Over the course of time, a melding of these languages occurred. And along with this, came a new national identity and pride. The inhabitants of England no longer thought of themselves as *Saxons* or *Frenchmen* but as *Englishmen.*

By the time Henry V reestablished English as the official language of the land around 1400, English was evolving into a new and extremely exciting vehicle for communication. New words and new ways of saying things became the mark of a clever person.

It was into this atmosphere that Shakespeare was born. By the time Shakespeare had come along, language was not merely a tool used to get through the day, but a song to be sung, a flag to be waved, capable of expressing anything and everything. It was a kind of national sport. The basic rules had been laid down and now the sky was the limit. Everyone was a *rapper,* a *wordsmith.* And Shakespeare was better at this game than anyone of his time and perhaps since. It is said that Shakespeare added over a thousand *new* words to the language.

Getting *easy* with Shakespeare is like learning to read or drive; once you get the hang of it, your world is changed.

Language is the *guardian* at the entrance gate to the land of Shakespeare. To enter, one must tame the guardian. This simply means that you must take the time to become familiar with his ways.

And now for the good news, once you learn the guardian's way, he changes. He ceases to be an obstacle and instead becomes your guide and ally; your conveyance to Shakespeare's world and mind.

Let's examine a few of the techniques that will help you to tame the guardian and make your exploration of Shakespeare easier.

1) The first thing to do is to find out what all the words mean. In order to do this, you will want to go to your local library and gather any Shakespeare lexicons or glossaries, and as many different dictionaries and thesauri you can locate, along with all the versions of *Romeo and Juliet* (with their various footnotes and explanations) and look up all the words you don't know. Note their various meanings and try to determine which best fits the context you found the word in.

2) We must remember that Shakespeare, as well as other poets, took *poetic license*—they will allow themselves to deviate from accepted form in order to achieve a desired effect. Poets will often rearrange words to acheive a more musical, poetical structure, or perhaps to get a rhyme to occur at the end of a line. Sometimes, by merely rearranging the subject, verb, adverbs, etc., into the order we are used to today, we can clarify the meaning of an otherwise complicated sentence.

For example, the Friar's line:

"Hear me a little speak"

in Act 3 scene 3, can be clarified by rearranging the words to read:

"Hear me speak a little,"

or Juliet's line in Act 3 scene 5:

"tell my lady I am gone, having displeased my father, to Laurence's cell"

becomes clear when we invert the words to:

"having displeased my father, tell my lady I am gone to Friar Laurence's cell."

3) Another thing Shakespeare does, is to take words and *stretch* their obvious meanings. He will use a word in a correct, but somewhat unusual manner so that he makes us see something in a whole new light and thereby broadens and enrichens our view of the world. When Montague sees Romeo dead and says:

"O thou untaught! What manners is in this, to *press* before thy father to a grave?"

Shakespeare is stretching the usual meaning of the word *press.* He uses it in such a way as to create the image of Romeo rushing headlong through the generations and pushing his way to death.

Another example of this is in Act 3 scene 1 when Benvolio tells the Prince,

"O noble Prince, I can *discover* all."

The word *discover* usually implies finding something new, but if we allow ourselves to stretch its meaning, we realize that Benvolio is talking about *uncovering the truth of events.*

When we come across a situation like this, we must look at the context of the unusual usage and use our imaginations to stretch the meanings of the word as Shakespeare might have done. Once we start thinking like Shakespeare, we can open ourselves to the various shades of meaning contained in words.

4) Shakespeare's use of the apostrophe sometimes makes words seem strange to us, but when we realize that he is using it no differently than we do in modern English, the words become easy to understand.

An apostrophe merely tells us that there is something missing–for example, in the word "I'll"–the apostrophe replaces the "wi" –"I'll" is a contraction for "I will." So with Shakespeare, the word "o'er" means "over." Shakespeare often contracts words in this manner to alter the number of syllables in a line in order to fit his poetic structure.

5) Yet another thing to keep in mind when dealing with Shakespeare, is that most of the punctuation in the versions you will read was put there by an editor in subsequent centuries and was not Shakespeare's.

Quite frankly, Shakespeare was more concerned with meaning than with grammatically correct punctuation. He was writing for actors and his objective with punctuation was to clarify how an actor should interpret a line. In fact, it is thought that many of the actors in Shakespeare's company could not read and that the learning of a script was a verbal process.

Therefore, a good way to get more comfortable with Shakespeare might be to listen to professional actors on recordings of Shakespeare's plays and follow along in a script. Don't be afraid to imitate what you hear, it is an excellent way to learn.

6) We find though, that the very best way to become comfortable with Shakespeare and his language is to work with the material *out loud.* There is something marvelous that happens when we speak the words that helps to clarify their meanings.

Merely reading about baseball rarely improves your technique–so with Shakespeare, his material was

meant to be *performed,* and therefore, the best way to connect to and understand the material is to speak it out loud, preferably with other people, but even alone works wonders.

You'll be amazed to discover Shakespeare's language becoming clearer and clearer as you work this way. Just remember; patience and practice!

# Taming the guardian
### (an exercise to help understand Shakespeare's language)

This exercise is designed to put into practice the various techniques for understanding Shakespeare that we have just talked about.

Select one of the following speeches (which are from *Romeo and Juliet* and have either been cut or not used in their entirety in our version of the play) and *translate* the speech into vernacular American.

This is the time to go to the library and locate all those reference books that we talked about earlier and look up all the words in the speech you've chosen.

You might want to do this working as a group or in pairs, sharing your ideas as you work. Or, you might work individually on the same speech and then compare results after.

Once you have found the various meanings of the words, and made lists of them, you can begin to select the ones that seem most appropriate for conveying the meaning of the speech.

Note that you may also need to rearrange the order of words to clarify the meaning.

Now put this all together and write a vernacular version of the speech. When doing this, try to imagine the words that the character who speaks the speech in the play, might use if he or she were speaking today.

Remember, there are no right or wrong ways to do this exercise. Be creative and daring. Shakespeare certainly would be if he were around today and had our version of the English language to work with!

Now that you have broken the code and the guardian is starting to seem friendlier, go back to the original version of your speech and read it aloud keeping strongly in mind the meanings of the words that you have now discovered.

Note how much clearer Shakespeare's language has become for you and for your listeners. This is the fact that every actor knows; *the clearer the under-*

*standing of the language, the more clearly it will be conveyed.*

Note too, how well Shakespeare says things—in such a way that pretty much sums it up. It is not only the words he chooses, but the order he has selected to put them in, that creates the incredibly rich imagery that he is so famous for. You could say it differently perhaps, but not better!

*This is why, while it is possible to update the language, with vernacular versions, it is certainly never preferable to use them for any reason other than as a tool for getting back to the original.*

He is the *Master!*—and now that you are learning how to tame the guardian, you will be able to enter into Shakespeare's world and begin to discover the breadth and depth of his insights into human nature.

[You will note that for this exercise, we have printed Shakespeare's text in *verse form*. This is the way you will find Shakespeare's works commonly printed. We have chosen not to use the verse form in our cut version for reasons of simplicity, but now that you have become more familiar with Shakespeare and his language, it might be a good idea to get used to it. When dealing with the verse form, do not stop at the end of the line unless there is punctuation telling you to. If there is not a period or a colon, continue reading on until the thought is complete. Also, don't be thrown by the fact that each line begins with a capitalized letter, this is merely part of the form.]

Montague: (Act 1 scene 1, explaining to Benvolio how strangely Romeo has been acting recently)
> ...all so soon as the all-cheering sun
> Should in the farthest east begin to draw
> The shady curtains from Aurora's bed,
> Away from light steals home my heavy son,
> And private in his chamber pens himself,
> Shuts up his windows, locks fair daylight out,
> And makes himself an artificial night.
> Black and portentous must this humour prove,
> Unless good counsel may the cause remove.

Romeo: (Act 1 scene 1, discussing his opinion of love's qualities—pre-Juliet)
> Love is a smoke made with the fume of sighs;
> Being purged, a fire sparkling in lovers' eyes;
> Being vexed, a sea nourished with loving tears:
> What is it else? a madness most discreet,
> A choking gall, and a preserving sweet.

Romeo: (Act 1 scene 1, describing Rosaline's *armor* against love)
> she hath Dian's wit;
> And, in strong proof of chastity well armed,
> From love's weak childish bow she lives unharmed.
> She will not stay the siege of loving terms,
> Nor bide the encounter of assailing eyes,
> Nor ope her lap to saint-seducing gold:
> O, she is rich in beauty; only poor,
> That, when she dies, with beauty dies her store.

Sampson: (Act 1 scene 2, puzzling over the written words that he can't make heads nor tails of—note that all his examples are confused—straighten them out for him)
> It is written that the shoemaker should meddle with his yard, and the tailor with his last, the fisher with his pencil, and the painter with his nets; but I am sent to find those persons, whose names are here writ, and can never find what names the writing person hath here writ. I must to the learned!

[note that Shakespeare has written this speech in prose, he often mixes prose and verse within the same play, depending on the status of the speaker]

Benvolio: (Act 1 scene 2, telling Romeo that he thinks Rosaline best because he has not compared her to other woman)
> Tut! You saw her fair, none else being by
> Herself poised with herself in either eye:
> But in that crystal scales, let there be weighted
> Your lady's love against some other maid
> That I will show you, shining at this feast,
> And she shall scant show well, that now shows best.

Nurse: (Act 1 scene 3, pointing out how she remembers Juliet's age)
> Of all days in the year, come Lammas-eve at night, shall she be fourteen. Susan and she—God rest all Christian souls—were of an age—well, Susan is with God, she was too good for me. But as I said, on Lammas-eve at night shall she be fourteen, that shall she marry, I remember it well.

[Remember: the Nurse was hired because she had recently given birth herself and therefore could breast-feed Juliet. Susan was her child.]

Romeo: (Act 1 scene 5, upon seeing Juliet for the first time—comparing her beauty to other girls)

She doth teach the torches to burn bright!
It seems she hangs upon the cheek of night
As a rich jewel in an Ethiop's ear:
Beauty too rich for use, for earth too dear!
So shows a snowy dove trooping with crows,
As yonder lady o'er her fellows shows.

Capulet: (Act 1 scene 5, telling Tybalt how to treat Romeo at the feast)

I would not for the wealth of all this town,
Here in my house, do him disparagement:
Therefore be patient, take no note of him,
It is my will; the which if thou respect,
Show a fair presence, and put off these frowns,
An ill-beseeming semblance for a feast.

Romeo: (Act 2 scene 2, seeing Juliet at her window noting how she outshines everything around her)

But soft, what light through yonder window
    breaks?
It is the east, and Juliet is the sun!
Arise fair sun and kill the envious moon,
Who is already sick and pale with grief,
That thou her maid art far more fair than she.

Romeo: (Act 2 scene 2, comparing the luminosity of Juliet's eyes to twinkling stars—Juliet is the clear winner in Romeo's book!)

Two of the fairest stars in all the heaven,
Having some business, do entreat her eyes
To twinkle in their spheres till they return.
What if her eyes were there, they in her head?
The brightness of her cheek would shame those
    stars,
As daylight doth a lamp; her eye in heaven
Would through the airy region stream so bright,
That birds would sing, and think it were not night.

Romeo: (Act 2 scene 2, Juliet has asked Romeo by whose direction he found her window—remember, love—Cupid—is said to be blind)

By love, that first did prompt me to inquire;
He lent me counsel, and I lent him eyes.
I am no pilot, yet wert thou as far
As that vast shore washed with the farthest sea,
I should adventure for such merchandise.

Juliet: (Act 2 scene 2, telling Romeo that while she is less coy than other girls, she is definitely more loyal)

        if thou think'st I am too quickly won,
I'll frown, and be perverse, and say thee nay,
So thou wilt woo; but, else not for the world.

In truth, fair Montague, I am too fond,
And therefore thou may'st think my 'havior light:
But trust me, gentleman, I'll prove more true
Than those that have more cunning to be strange.

Friar Laurence: (Act 2 scene 3, discussing the different sleep patterns of the old and the young)

Care keeps his watch in every old man's eye,
And where care lodges, sleep will never lie:
But where unbruised youth with unstuffed brain
Doth couch his limbs, there golden sleep doth
    reign.

Friar Laurence: (Act 2 scene 3, scolding Romeo for being so fickle about women)

Holy Saint Francis! What a change is here!
Is Rosaline, that thou did'st love so dear,
So soon forsaken? Young men's love then lies,
Not truly in their hearts, but in their eyes.
Jesu Maria! what a deal of brine
Hath washed thy sallow cheeks for Rosaline!
How much salt water thrown away in waste,
To season love, that of it doth not taste!

Juliet: (Act 2 scene 5, wishing she could have had a faster messenger than the Nurse to bring her Romeo's news)

O, she is lame! Love's heralds should be thought,
Which ten times faster glide than the sun's beams,
Driving back shadows over lowring hills.

Nurse: (Act 2 scene 5, finally telling Juliet Romeo's news)

Then hie you hence to Friar Laurence' cell,
There stays a husband to make you a wife;
Now comes the wanton blood up in your cheeks,
They'll be in scarlet straight at any news.
Hie you to church; I must another way,
To fetch a ladder, by the which your love
Must climb a bird's nest soon, when it is dark:
I am the drudge, and toil in your delight;
But you shall bear the burden soon at night.

Romeo: (Act 2 scene 6, asking Juliet to put into words, if she can, the extreme joy they feel in each other's company)

Ah Juliet, if the measure of thy joy
Be heaped like mine, and that thy skill be more
To blazon it, then sweeten with thy breath
This neighbor air, and let rich music's tongue,
Unfold the imagined happiness that both
Receive in either, by this dear encounter.

Mercutio: (Act 3 scene 1, ironically making fun of Benvolio's peaceful nature by accusing him of being a hell-raiser)

> Thou art like one of these fellows that, when he
> enters the confines of a tavern, claps me his
> sword upon the table, and says, "God send me no
> need of thee!" and by the operation of the second
> cup, draws him on the drawer, when indeed there
> is no need.

Prince: (Act 3 scene 1, telling the Capulets and the Montagues that they will both be made to suffer for Mercutio's death)

> I have an interest in your hates' proceeding,
> My blood for your rude brawls doth lie a bleeding;
> But I'll amerce you with so strong a fine,
> That you shall all repent the loss of mine:
> I will be deaf to pleading and excuses;
> Nor tears, nor prayers, shall purchase out abuses,
> Therefore use none.

Juliet: (Act 3 scene 2, musing on Romeo's incredible qualities)

> and, when he shall die,
> Take him and cut him out in little stars,
> And he will make the face of heaven so fine,
> That all the world will be in love with night,
> And pay no worship to the garish sun.

Juliet: (Act 3 scene 2, trying to understand who is dead when the Nurse is going on about death—note that "I" also meant *ay* which means *yes*)

> Hath Romeo slain himself? say thou but *I*,
> And that bare vowel *I* shall poison more
> Than the death-darting eye of cockatrice:
> I am not I, if there be such an *I;*
> Or those eyes shut, that make thee answer, *I.*
> If he be slain, say—*I;* or if not—no:
> Brief sounds determine of my weal, or woe.

Romeo: (Act 3 scene 3, telling the friar what "banishment" means to him)

> There is no world without Verona walls,
> But purgatory, torture, hell itself.
> Hence banished is banished from the world,
> And world's exile is death:—then banished
> Is death mis-termed: calling death, banishment,
> Thou cut'st my head off with a golden axe,
> And smil'st upon the stroke that murders me.

Capulet: (Act 3 scene 4, asking Paris if he is amenable to having the wedding on Thursday)

> Will you be ready? do you like this haste?
> We'll keep no great ado—a friend or two—
> For hark you, Tybalt being slain so late,
> It may be thought we held him carelessly,
> Being our kinsman, if we revel much:
> Therefore we'll have some half a dozen friends,
> And there an end. But what say you to Thursday?

Juliet: (Act 3 scene 5, when Romeo has left her, begging *fortune* to send faithful Romeo back to her quickly)

> O fortune, fortune! all men call thee fickle:
> If thou art fickle, what dost thou with him,
> That is renowned for faith? Be fickle, fortune;
> For then, I hope, thou wilt not keep him long,
> But send him back.

Capulet: (Act 3 scene 5, thinking Juliet is still crying over Tybalt's death and comparing her crying to a boat tossed about on a wild sea)

> How now! a conduit, girl? What, still in tears?
> Evermore showering? In one little body
> Thou conterfeit'st a bark, a sea, a wind:
> For still thy eyes, which I may call the sea,
> Do ebb and flow with tears; the bark, thy body is,
> Sailing in this salt flood; the winds, thy sighs;
> Who, raging with thy tears, and they with them,
> Without a sudden calm, will overset
> Thy tempest-tossed body.

Capulet: (Act 3 scene 5, furious that Juliet should reject Paris after all that he has done to find him)

> Day, night, hour, tide, time, work, play,
> Alone, in company, still my care hath been
> To have her matched: and having now provided
> A gentleman of noble parentage,
> Of fair demesnes, youthful, and nobly trained,
> Stuffed (as they say) with honorable parts,
> Proportioned as one's heart could wish a man,—
> And then to have a wretched puling fool,
> A whining mammet, in her fortune's tender,
> To answer—"I'll not wed, I cannot love,
> I am too young,—I pray you, pardon me."

Juliet: (Act 4 scene 1, telling Friar Laurence she will kill herself if he cannot help her avoid a marriage to Paris)

> If, in thy wisdom, thou canst give no help,
> Do thou but call my resolution wise,
> And with this knife I'll help it presently.
> God joined my heart and Romeo's, thou our
> hands;

And ere this hand, by thee to Romeo sealed,
Shall be the label to another deed,
Or my true heart with treacherous revolt
Turn to another, this shall slay them both.

Juliet: (Act 4 scene 4, having second thoughts as she is about to drink the potion)
What if it be a poison, which the friar
Subtly hath ministered to have me dead;
Lest in this marriage he should be dishonored,
Because he married me before to Romeo?
I fear it is: and yet, methinks it should not,
For he hath still been tried a holy man.
I will not entertain so bad a thought.

Romeo: (Act 5 scene 3, seeing Juliet in the Capulet tomb)
Ah, dear Juliet,
Why art thou yet so fair? Shall I believe
That unsubstantial death is amorous;
And that the lean abhorred monster keeps
Thee here in dark to be his paramour?
For fear of that, I still will stay with thee;
And never from this palace of dim night
Depart again.

# Queen Mab
## (an examination of Shakespeare's use of imagery)

In Shakespeare's time there were no televisions, no videos, and no films. Shakespeare did not have the option of working with a cameraman who could pan across a field of wildflowers, up the softly, sloping hills to a grove of birch trees through which we would see the sun beginning to make its first appearance of the day. No! Shakespeare had only the words of the English language to work with and so he said:

"the sun peered forth the golden window of the east"

With these words, Shakespeare paints a word-picture of the sun beginning to rise in the crystal clear eastern sky. He makes us see the sun just peeking over the horizon and we get the idea of the sky as the window through which the sun is shining its golden rays on us. This is one of the many examples of Shakespeare's incredibly rich imagery.

The "Queen Mab" speech, as it is known, is a another example of this. This is a speech of Mercutio's which we've cut in our version of the play but which we would like to explore here.

Preceeding the Queen Mab speech, Romeo has told Mercutio that he has dreamt a dream that is very disturbing to him. Romeo indicates that he believes dreams to be valid predictors of the future. With his Queen Mab speech, Mercutio is trying to convince Romeo that dreams are merely figments of the imagination and therefore should not be taken so seriously. Mercutio says:

"O then, I see Queen Mab hath been with you.
She is the *fairies' midwife;* and she comes
In shape no bigger than *an agate-stone*
On *the fore-finger of an alderman,*
Drawn with *a team of little atomies*
Over men's noses as they lie asleep.
Her waggon-spokes made of *long spinners' legs;*
The cover, of *the wings of grasshoppers;*
Her traces, of *the smallest spider's web;*
Her collars, of *the moonshine's wat'ry beams;*
Her whip, of *cricket's bone;* the lash, of *film;*
Her waggoner, *a small grey-coated gnat,*
Not half so big as *a round little worm*
Pricked from *the lazy finger of a maid:*
Her chariot is *an empty hazel-nut,*
Made by *the joiner squirrel,* or *old grub,*
Time out of mind *the fairies' coach-makers.*
And in this state she gallops night by night
Through lovers' brains, and then they dream of love."

Here we have imagery that Walt Disney would be mighty proud of. Shakespeare has created a little creature, Queen Mab, who he tells us is as tiny as *an agate-stone.* How tiny is that? An agate-stone is a small semi-precious stone that is carved in the shape of a tiny figure (like a cameo) and placed in a setting to be worn as a ring. Shakespeare goes on to pin-point the size of this particular agate-stone by telling us that it is like the ones aldermen wear on their index fingers. An alderman was a member of the city council, so this would indicate to us that Queen Mab is not as tiny as the stone a baker's wife might wear on her finger, yet not as large as one that the Prince might have on.

Shakespeare describes Queen Mab as *the fairies' midwife.* This tells us that she is a member of fairyland. This covers a whole range of magical, mythical creatures who inhabit the other-worldly realms which were imagined both in Shakespeare's day and which we can still relate to today. A *midwife* is someone who assists in the process of giving birth. In this case, Shakespeare is talking about giving birth to dreams.

Queen Mab is then the member of the fairy world who helps humans to bring forth their dreams. (Does she like her work? How old is she? How is she dressed?)

Shakespeare goes on to describe the wagon that she is riding in. He tells us that it is pulled by *a team of little atomies.* The word *atomi* in Shakespeare's time referred to the smallest creature imaginable—so rather than miniature horses, Shakespeare chooses a team of atomies to pull this tiny coach. (What do these tiny creatures look like?)

He then proceeds to tell us that the spokes of the wheels are made of *long spinners' legs.* A spinner is a spider who spins webs, and in this case, Shakespeare is telling us that the spokes are made of the legs of long-legged spiders or daddy long-legs!

The wagon's covering is made from *grasshopper's wings.* (How are they attached? Are they opaque or can you see light through them?) The traces, (which are parts of the harnesses for the *atomies*) are made of small *spider webs.* (Are the spider webs collected from baby spiders and then spun into thread on miniature spinning wheels that is then used to make harnesses?)

The collars, (another part of the harnesses) are made of *the moonshine's watery beams.* (Are these beams of light that the moon emits on a foggy night that then become heavy with the moisture in the fog? And is Shakespeare suggesting that this substance can be harnessed to make harness parts? and do you suppose this stuff glows in the dark?)

Queen Mab carries a whip, the handle of which is made of the *bone of a cricket* (which particular bone do you think is used?) and the lash is made of *film.* *Film* in Shakespeare's day was the membrane of a seed pod. (Snap the top of a green bean and pull the string—are a bunch of these strings tied together to make the *lash?* What sound does the *lash* make when it's popped over the *atomies* backs?)

To drive this tiny vehicle, Queen Mab has hired a rather dapperly-dressed, teen-age gnat. (At least *small* may indicate that he's still a teenager, or perhaps he's just very short!) In any case, his grey suit sounds very spiffy. (Do you suppose it's a tuxedo?) Shakespeare is pretty insistent about his tininess, stressing that he is not half as big as *a round little worm* which has been removed from the finger of a lazy maid. There was a saying in Shakespeare's day that suggested that worms bred on idle hands and here Shakespeare is suggesting that the gnat who drove Queen Mab's coach was only

half as big as one of the tiny worms that could be picked of *the lazy finger of a maid.*

The chariot (wagon) itself has been constructed using an *empty hazelnut* shell, by *the joiner squirrel* or the *old grub.* A joiner was a furniture-maker, and obviously squirrels or old grubs (which are insects, proficient at boring holes in wood) were the best furniture-makers in fairyland.

So that what we have here, is a tiny fairy, named Queen Mab, who rides around throughout the night, in a wonderfully appointed little carriage, which was made by the fairies' coach-makers. The carriage is driven by a gnat wearing a grey coat and in it, Queen Mab goes galloping over sleeping men's noses and when she comes across a man in love, she gallops through his brain and makes him dream the *love-dream* that is in his thoughts waiting to come out.

## Queen Mab Exercise:

Using materials available to you, make a physical representation of some aspect of the Queen Mab speech. It can be a drawing, a sculpture, a collage etc. Use your imagination and create something that Shakespeare's imagery has made you see—whether it be some aspect of Queen Mab or the coach, or perhaps the workmen who make these tiny coaches. Whatever strikes your fancy—use your imagination and create!

When you have finished, compare your creations and note how many different images have arisen in your minds. Shakespeare's words have the power to spark our imaginations to new heights and new visions. This is the magic and power of his language.

# The rehearsal process
(who's who and what's what in putting a play together)

WHO'S WHO:

There is first of all the play, then the actors, then the director. The job of the director is to make sure the story gets told. This can entail many elements: working with actors to help them develop their characters, making sure each actor is headed in the right direction, maintaining order in the rehearsal so that work can move along smoothly, assigning people to do props, costumes etc.

The director is ultimately the benign dictator who makes sure everything comes together at the right time—that's why they get the big bucks!

The stage manager is the director's right hand—a combination of sergeant at arms and girl friday.

Among the stage manager's many jobs is: recording the blocking in a master script, prompting the actors when they forget their lines (that means a stage manager must always be following along in the script during rehearsals), making sure everyone is at rehearsal on time, coordinating the technical elements (props, costumes, etc.), calling break times and gathering everyone together after the break, helping the director maintain an orderly rehearsal, and once the show is in performance, the stage manager must make sure everyone and everything is in the proper place to insure the show will run smoothly, and most importantly, never becoming frazzled!

The stage manager can usually use an assistant or two. Give careful consideration when selecting someone for this position—a good stage manager is invaluable!

## CASTING THE PLAY:

The first thing we need to do is to *cast* the play; that is figure out who will play which role. This can be done by having *auditions* for the parts. To do this, people read various scenes from the play and then the director, teacher or the other members of the class make determinations of who would be best suited to play a certain role.

Another way to cast is to have the teacher assign roles. Sometimes it is fun to have multiple casts (more than one actor for each part) that way actors can share their ideas in rehearsal and learn from each other.

With multiple casting, the play could then be presented more times in order to give everyone a chance to *read* or perform. Note too, that a single actor might play two roles—this is known as *doubling.* For example, the actor who plays the chorus might come back as Friar John.

Something to keep in mind when casting, is that an obvious choice for a role may not always be the best one. Sometimes a male part might be better played by a female actor or visa versa. Or an actor whose physical characteristics are not exactly what's called for, might actually be able to bring something more interesting to a certain part. So remember to be flexible and open-minded in the casting process.

## INVESTIGATING THE SCRIPT:

Once the casting is determined, it's time to get to work. Professional actors usually begin the rehearsal process by sitting around together and reading the play out loud a number of times.

The first time through, we just listen to the story. The next time through we start discussing the play.

The rules here are usually that anyone may stop and ask a question at any time. It could be a question of the meaning of a word, a discussion of why a character does something, or perhaps a question about where a scene is taking place.

In other words, everything and anything that may not be perfectly clear should be examined at this point.

This is done to make sure that everyone fully understands what is being said and what is going on in the course of the play.

This can take days or even a week in a professional company (and that's working eight hours a day!) So take your time on this step and be thorough.

The more time spent clarifying everything at this stage of the process, the more smoothly the rest of the rehearsal will go.

Once all the questions have been answered, go back and read the play again and note how much richer and clearer the language will be to you.

At this point the decision must be made whether you are going to do a *reading* of the play or a simple production. A reading is a modified performance in which there would be no sets or costumes and is usually done with only the simplest movement. Actors could just be seated in a semicircle, facing the listeners, with their scripts in hand and read the play.

## DOING A READING:

If you have decided upon a reading, you still must determine how best to tell the story of the play to make it clear and interesting for the audience.

This is done by adding *shape* or *structure* to our work. We do this by going scene-by-scene through the play and (having determined what the scene is about in our previous work) figuring out how it fits into the overall *arc* of the play, how that scene moves the story forward and how each character contributes to that movement.

By examining the scenes in this way, we can then determine the *rhythms* that the scene requires for the acting of it: for example, some will need to be fast-paced, some slow, some a combination of both; some will need to be quiet, some raucous; in some, the characters will speak quickly—perhaps overlapping the previous speaker, and in others, the language will be languid or perhaps romantic.

All these various elements will add what we refer to as *shape* and *color* to the material.

We do this with each scene and slowly expand our work to include larger sections, till the entire shape of the play becomes clear. Experiment, explore and see what works best for your production.

The director makes the final decisions because he or she will have the best overview of the play, having been able to watch it all.

The most important element for a reading is a clear understanding of the language, the situation (or story) and the character relationships. These are after all, the most critical elements of Shakespeare.

This would be an excellent place for most classes to get to. But for those of you who wish to do a simple staging of the play, read on.

BLOCKING:

If you have decided to stage a production of the play, you still must do all the work of shaping discussed in the reading section, only you do this while *blocking* the play.

Blocking is the process of organizing the physical movement of the play. We usually block working one scene at a time and holding our scripts (that is before beginning to memorize our lines.)

The reason we do this, is because most actors find it much easier to memorize lines when the lines are connected to movements. (Note that the blocking we have offered with the text is merely one way to go, feel free to create movement that feels comfortable for you.)

WORKING SCENES AND MEMORIZING:

The next step would be to *work scenes* of the play—that is to rehearse them, adjusting the blocking as needed to make sure the actors feel comfortable with the movement and checking that the situations in the text are being properly clarified. It is during this step that we also begin memorizing the lines.

Memorization usually begins to happen on its own at this point, particularly if all the previous discussion work has been thoroughly accomplished. Shakespeare writes so well that his words seem to become the only ones to say in the situations that he has devised. This is not the case with all playwrights!

There are times though (particularly with longer speeches) when it is necessary to go over and over a section out loud until it is ingrained in the brain and in the muscles of the mouth. (It's amazing how many times on stage, an actor has forgotten a line but his or her mouth still keeps going and knows what to say!) If an actor forgets a line during rehearsal, he or she says the word "line" and the stage manager (who is follow-ing along in the script) reads the line to the actor and work goes on.

This period of rehearsal is the longest and most exciting part of the process. It is when we go over and over each scene, that the language and the actions truly become part of us and we grow to understand a little more about the characters and their situations each time through. It is over this period that it is often said we are *becoming* the character.

In a professional situation, we are lucky if we have four weeks to spend on this part of the process. So again, spend as much time as you can.

Once individual scenes begin to *take shape,* we start putting together larger chunks of the play. Perhaps doing three or four scenes in a row and beginning to feel the *flow* of the play and finding the *throughline* of the characters.

Don't forget that this is an ongoing process and that different actors have creative inspirations at different points in the rehearsal period.

If someone comes up with a new and exciting idea after blocking has been completed, experiment with it and be willing to change, if it turns out to be better.

This is the *creative process* and these are the very instincts and ideas that will make your production unique and wonderful.

RUN-THROUGHS:

It is at this point that we put the whole play together and go through it from beginning to end. It is during the *run-throughs* that we finally get to understand what is needed from us as actors to take our character from his or her starting place to where they end up in the play.

TECHS AND DRESSES:

It is now that we add the final elements of props and costumes (sometimes, we are lucky enough to have gotten these earlier in our rehearsal process and have been able to incorporate them sooner.) But we definitely need everything at this point! These are referred to as the *technical* elements of the production.

Remember, though that the ultimate element of any Shakespearean production is the incredibly wonderful language through which Shakespeare conveys his ideas. Keep it simple and clear and it will enlighten and uplift...Good show!

# Developing a Character
## (an exercise for creating a character history)

When working on a play, an actor will usually create a *history* or *background* for his or her character. This is the story of the character's life. It is made up by the actor in order to gather insights into the character's psyche and better understand how that character will respond to the various situations that he or she is confronted with in the course of a play.

We create this story by examining the *givens* in the text (that is, the various hints that the playwright has written into or given in the script), and making lists of all the information that we gather.

These include:

A) Everything that is said about the character by other characters in the play.

B) Everything the characters says about him or herself.

C) An examination of the physical characteristics and the physical limitations that the playwright might have specified in the text.

In addition to this information, we get more by asking a series of questions about the character:

1) what does the character want? This is a twofold question:

a) What does the character want in the big picture of life–does he or she want to be a movie star? to be rich? to be loved?

b) What does the character want in each scene? In other words, what is he or she desiring the other characters to do or say?

2) How does the character go about getting those things?–does the character aggressively go after things or is he or she passive? will she "sell her grandmother"? is he honest and plodding?

3) How does the character react in various situations–with anger? passively? with compassion? etc.

4) How does the character feel about him or herself?

5) What is his or her environment or social situation? Is this character from a family of fourteen and ignored by everyone? is he or she from a big city? a small town? a rich family? a well-educated family? etc.

6) How does the character's mind operate? Is he or she quick-witted or slow? plodding or inventive? etc.

7) What is the character's journey through the play? In other words, what is that character like when we first encounter them and when and how does the character evolve, grow or change during the course of the play? Or does that character remain unchanged?

We find the answers to these questions by scouring the text and by *creating* answers with our imaginations when they are not available. This is precisely why no two actors can ever play a character the same way. Each actor has personally created that character!

We now take the *givens* we have discovered in the text and combine these with the various answers we have come up with to our series of questions and create from this raw material our character's history.

During rehearsal, we constantly refer back to this history to help us figure out our character's actions and responses to the various situations in the play.

Remember, there are no right or wrong ways to do this. Just be honest in your search and when in doubt, always go back to the text.

# Acting techniques and theatrical conventions

For those of you considering doing a performance of the play, here are some basic acting techniques and theatrical conventions to keep in mind.

PACING SHAKESPEARE'S PLAYS:

In Shakespeare's day, it is generally agreed that his plays were performed with alacrity. The language moved and the action moved.

With Shakespeare, perhaps more than with any other playwright, there is an acting technique that dictates that as soon as the last line of one scene is spoken, the first line of the next scene comes in hot on its tail.

Language is, after all the critical element of Shakespeare and we want all the action to come *on the language*–that is, with the words–unless otherwise specified. This means that when a stage direction says 'enter UL X DC' it means that the language begins at the entrance unless otherwise specified. Also, whenever possible, actors should be moving towards their exit with their last lines so that the action and language are continuous.

This does not mean that the actor has to feel rushed or be afraid to take pauses, it's just that for the most part, Shakespeare is best performed without indulgence. As Hamlet says to the players:

"Speak the speech I pray you, as I pronounced it to you, *trippingly* on the tongue."

## STAGE ETIQUETTE:

Another important element for our purposes in performing, requires that after exiting from the stage, an actor proceed quietly and unobtrusively around upstage to the next place where he or she will make an entrance and then silently watch the action on stage until it is time to reenter.

Courtesy and cooperation are two of the most important elements in the theatre. We work as a team and do all we can to assist our fellow actors and thereby help our production move along smoothly. This means, for example, that when Juliet has her very fast exit and entrance between act 3 scene 5 and act 4 scene 1, and she quickly has to move from SL up and around to SR, everyone clears back and makes room for her.

## MONOLOGUES:

If your character has a monologue, you have some choices in how to deliver it.

Depending on the situation, you could either talk directly to the audience and share your *inner thoughts* with them, or you could do the speech as though you were *thinking out loud* and the audience is overhearing you.

In Act 2 scene 3, Friar Laurence could chose either way to do his monologue.

## ASIDES:

An *aside* is a bit of dialogue that the audience hears, but supposedly, the other characters on stage do not hear.

Romeo's line;

"Is she a Capulet? O dear, my foe!"

in Act 1 scene 4 is an example of an aside.

These are usually best executed by the actor who has the aside saying it directly to the audience and the other actors going on about their business as though they don't hear it.

## ANGLING OUT:

This is a theatrical convention for making sure that the audience can see the actors onstage.

In real life when two people talk to each other, they probably stand face-to-face, but on stage it is necessary to stand on an angle facing slightly out to the audience in order to be seen.

When standing on the sides of the stage it is often necessary for the actor who is nearest the outside to place him or herself a little below and on an angle to the actor who is closer to the center in order to make sure the audience can see the action.

This is definitely something to experiment with.

## COUNTERING:

Countering is adjusting your position on stage to accommodate or balance a movement made by another actor: such as when someone joins a scene already in progress or when an actor is required to cross from one side of you to the other.

We do this in order to keep adequate spacing between the actors on stage so that the audience can get a clear view of the action.

## LIGHTING/DARKNESS:

In Shakespeare's day, most of the performances of his plays were done during the day in an open air theater. Therefore, night (darkness) was established by the language of the playwright and by various actor *conventions.*

Darkness can be *established* by the actor staring wide-eyed to show how hard it is to see at night, or feeling around with arms extended to indicate the difficulty of maneuvering in the dark.

Unsure, tentative movement, tripping or knocking into things also establishes the situation. This can be done either comically or straightforwardly depending upon the effect desired.

This does not mean that the actor has to concentrate on this during the entire scene. It is usually established when he or she first enters into the scene and then the actors returns to more normal actions and perhaps just reestablishes it from time to time.

## SOUND EFFECTS/OFFSTAGE MUSIC:

Again, getting back to Shakespeare's day, there were no tape recorders. Sound effects were done by the actors offstage, or sometimes onstage as the case may be.

We suggest for our purposes that we follow Shakespeare's lead and perform our sound effects in this manner.

In Act 3 scene 5 when the Friar hears a noise, this would be made by the Watch—perhaps ad libbing some sounds having tripped over a gravestone!

When Capulet calls for music to play at the party, it would be great if someone who plays the flute, recorder or perhaps a guitar could be offstage way down left, and *softly* play "Greensleeves" or some other Elizabethan—sounding piece in the background which would end just before Juliet enters, cooling off, after the dance.

## AD LIBS:

When the term *ad lib* is noted in a script, it indicates to the actor that he or she must make up some words or dialogue to fill the moment.

In Act 3 scene 1 when Benvolio is required to ad lib during the Mercutio—Tybalt fight, he might throw in, "Hold!" "Mercutio!" "Peace!"

Remember that whenever an ad lib is called for, it must be appropriate to the character and to the time in which that character lived!

## THUMB-BITE:

This was an insulting gesture which was similar to our present-day *shooting the finger.* It was executed by placing one's thumb-nail behind one's upper front teeth and flicking the thumb outward to produce a sound. While different from our current-day gesture, it had the same effect on the person to whom it was directed.

## STAMPS/KNOCKING:

Stamping on the floor is a *theatrical convention* actors use when there are no actual doors present on a set. If an actor merely stamps with the same intention and attitude as he would knock on a door, the audience will immediately accept this convention.

## PANTOMIME:

The pantomime of Juliet's burial is what was called a *dumb show* in Shakespeare's day. All the action takes place without speaking.

Because there are no words, gestures become more important—but be careful! The gestures and actions should be appropriate and not be over-exaggerated. For example, when Lady Capulet sees Juliet dead, she should take time to register the fact and then simply turn to her husband and put her head on his shoulder. Capulet should then merely gesture to Sampson and Gregory and they cross to Juliet, lift her up as gracefully as possible and lead the others out. Remember to rehearse the lift of Juliet enough so that the move is safe and can be executed smoothly and with dignity.

The idea of this dumb-show is that as Balthasar tells Romeo about the news of Juliet's death and burial, this is what Romeo is seeing in his mind's eye and causes him to make his final and fatal decision.

When rehearsing this scene, go slowly and be careful—and *don't* drop Juliet, she needs to be there for the curtain call! As you become more comfortable with the moves, it should begin to resemble a solemn march or processional.

## SWORDFIGHTS/FIGHTING:

In the history of theatre, there have probably been more actors hurt during sword fights than at any other time on stage. Stage combat is supposed to create an illusion of fighting, not recreate the real thing!

In a full-scale production, hundreds of hours of painstaking (and pain-avoiding) rehearsals are spent working on fights with a fight-master and a fight-captain who are constantly drilling actors to avoid accidents. Even then, someone will have a bad day and either give or get an injury.

Since the purpose of this endeavor is to shake hands with Shakespeare and not get stabbed by him, we suggest extreme care and simplicity in dealing with the fights.

To begin with, real swords should not be used. Yard sticks or thin wooden curtain dowling with a crosspiece attached with string to serve as a hilt (to help keep the *sword* in your belt) works very well.

The fights should be kept short and performed slowly. In fact slow motion fights have become a very popular theatrical convention in recent years. They are both dramatic and safe! One of the cardinal rules in theatre is *less is more,* this is particularly apt when it comes to swordfights!

In a fight of any kind onstage, nothing is left to chance or improvisation. Every move is meticulously worked out and rehearsed over and over again. A fight can be thought of as a dance between the two participants, with each dancer moving in unison with his or her partner.

The elements of any fight are the *attack* (the move made by the aggressor) and the *parry* (the counter move made by the other person to deflect). These moves are done in unison, with the person parrying the attack always knowing exactly where the attack is coming from.

The basic places to hit are:
1) the *top of the head*
   this blow is straight down at the head, the parry (or block) is done by holding the sword parallel to the floor above the head—at least 18" above the head.
2&3) these are *left and right shoulder cuts*
   they are parried by holding the sword at 90 degrees to the floor (with the blade upwards) and out to the side.
4&5) these are *right and left waist cuts*
   they are parried in the same manner as the shoul-

der cut but lower. Make sure that the waist cuts don't get lower than the waist.

6&7) these are *right and left thigh cuts*

they are parried by holding the sword 90 degrees to the ground and out to the side (tip down). Make sure to keep these cuts well below the waist– any confusion here can bring about the wrong parry.

8) *the thrust!* This is not a *blow,* but a *stab,* this is the final kill! *Remember–never directly at the person–always upstage or downstage!*

the parry for the thrust is similar to that of the waist cut. The blade should point upward and shove the thrusting blade away from you. Make sure a thrust is always chest high.

A sequence of three blows and then withdrawal (a return to your original position) is always good. For instance: 2-1-3 withdraw, or 3-1-2 withdraw, 3-7-3 withdraw, or 2-6-2 withdraw, etc. Go slowly and you will begin to see the possibilities emerge.

Three engagements of three blows each and then the *kill,* should be enough for all fights. The Romeo/Tybalt fight can be even shorter. In that fight, Romeo is so angry that he just flat powers Tybalt down and runs him through–nothing fancy at all.

In the fight in Act 1 scene 1, remember that the servants are not supposed to be good swordsmen. They mostly flail their blades, circling their opponents, rather than ever actually engaging in swordplay. Also note that once Tybalt and Benvolio start to fight–the servants probably just stand around and yell

encouragement to their guy while biting their thumbs at each other! It is no doubt the noise that they are making that brings on Capulet and Montague to investigate.

As far as the Tybalt/Benvolio fight is concerned, the uncut version of Benvolio's description of the fight provides some good clues–look it up.

With all fighting onstage, it's in the acting! *Act* stabbed and the audience will buy it! *And remember– safety first!*

JULIET'S STAB:

The important thing to remember here is that as the blow is delivered–collapse in on it. This gives the *impression* of killing oneself–and then Juliet will be able to take a curtain call!

# "Here's a marvelous convenient place for our rehearsal..."
## (a suggested set)

For our purposes, a simple set that serves for all locales is best.

We suggest a bare space. Entrances and exits need only be delineated by a strip of tape along the floor. When an actor crosses that line, he or she has *entered* or *exited* the stage.

Think of the stage with an imaginary diagonal running from UL to DR. Most of the Capulet action takes place in the section below that diagonal and most of the Montague action takes place above the diagonal.

The only set pieces needed are a short stool (or perhaps a wooden box) to sit upon and a ladder (no higher than five feet–for safety's sake) that can be mounted from either side.

With this and all other technical elements, simplicity is the key factor, because with Shakespeare, language is foremost! See page 126 for a set diagram.

# "Ay, those attires are best"
## (suggestions for costumes and props)

For our purposes, props and costumes should be kept to an absolute minimum.

This will not only make it easier to produce the play, but it will keep our focus firmly on the language where it needs to be.

### COSTUMES:

Since this play takes place in Italy, it might be appropriate to have the families dressed in red and green. Perhaps the Capulets in red shirts and the Montagues in green shirts.

Ladies might wear long or short dark-colored skirts. Men should wear jeans (with belts if they carry a sword).

The royal family members might wear purple shirts to signify their status.

The clergy could wear grey hooded-sweatshirts and sweat pants with long ropes tied at their waists.

Servants could wear t-shirts and upper class folks could wear long-sleeved shirts or blouses.

The Watchmen and the chorus could wear black shirts.

### PROPS:

Swords: covered in section on fights in acting technique chapter.

Vials: these could be small perfume bottles with corks—note that the one Friar Laurence gives to Juliet should be set in a non-traffic area DR at the top of the show.

Masks: these can be the plain black toy-store type masks, very simple!

Friar Laurence's basket: a simple basket with a handle

Rope: the rope the Nurse carries on is the supposed *rope-ladder*, but it need only be a coiled up rope for our needs since it is never used.

Torch: this could be a flashlight placed inside a milk container with cut-outs on it. Attach a cord to the top to carry it.

Daggers: both Romeo's and Juliet's should be the toy-store sort of rubber dagger.

Cloth: the cloth that Friar Laurence lays out for Juliet's body in the tomb can be a piece of colored fabric or a small blanket.

Letters and papers: simple enough!

Coins and money pouch: any coins will do! A little draw-string pouch with coins in it to give to Balthasar or a simple change purse.

# Glossary

THEATRICAL CONVENTION:
an agreed upon action (that may or may not be used in everyday life) which we *establish* on stage to convey something unusual that the script may require—for example:
stamping on floor to indicate knocking on an imaginary door thereby separating the onstage and offstage actor

ESTABLISH:
to *establish* is to set up a theatrical convention such as when Mercutio stamps on the floor in Act 1 scene 4 to indicate knocking on the Capulet's door. He has now established that stamping on the floor is equivalent to a door knock.

THEATRICAL LICENSE:
liberties we take with the script to achieve certain results that we as actors, directors or editors are going for.

BLOCKING:
the organized physical movement of a play.

REHEARSAL PROCESS:
the time between the casting of a play and the opening.

READING:
an organized, rehearsed presentation of a play in which the actors read from the script rather than memorizing the lines. (Could be done seated or with simple movements.)

SHAPE:
a clear definable beginning, middle and end to a scene or to the entire play. (Also referred to as *arc*.)

THROUGHLINE:
this usually refers to the series of actions a character performs throughout the course of a play in quest of his desires.

CUT:
In theatrical terms, to *cut* is to eliminate from the script.

VERNACULAR:
Vernacular is defined by Webster's as "using a language or dialect *native* to a region or country rather than a literary, cultured, or foreign lan-

guage." For our purposes then, vernacular would be our everyday American-English.

DOUBLING:

When one actor plays two parts, this is referred to as doubling. For example, whoever plays the Chorus at the very beginning of the play, might return as Friar John at the end.

STAGE:

the area designated as the space upon which the action of the play takes place.

ENTER:

to walk into the area referred to as the stage.

EXIT:

to leave the stage area.

CROSS: (often abbreviated "X")

to move across the stage to the area indicated by whatever stage direction follows the term. (xing then means—'crossing' in the stage directions)

STAGE TERMINOLOGY:

(note that the following stage terminology is indicated from the point of view of the actor, onstage, looking out to the audience)

SR:

the abbreviation for *stage right*. This means towards the right side of the stage as viewed by the actor when facing an audience.

SL:

the abbreviation for *stage left*—towards the left side of the stage from the actor's point of view.

US:

*upstage* means towards the rear of the stage.

DS:

*downstage* is towards the front of the stage.

C:

the *center* section of the stage.

We combine these terms to describe all the various sections of the stage. For example:

DRC: means *down-right-center* which refers to the lower part of the stage to the right of center stage.

DLC: *down-left-center* is the opposite of DRC.

UR: *upstage-right* is the upper part of the stage on the right side.

Use the chart following to determine other areas. Note that all areas are *approximate* designations only—this is not an exact science!

Use the chart at the back of the book to determine other designations.

# Additional Projects

1) Write out a list of adjectives that describe the various aspects of your character.

2) Play like Romeo and Juliet go to Capulet and tell him the truth about their marriage—what would that scene be like?

3) Make up the conversation that Abram and Balthasar are having when they approach the town square in the first scene.

4) Write out the story of what happens to your character during the entire course of the play when he or she is not onstage.

5) Act out the scene that took place at the Prince's between he and Montague and he and Capulet after the brawl in Act 1 scene 1.

6) Write a brief accounting of what might have happened if Capulet had not insisted that Juliet marry Paris.

7) Check out the time references in the play and figure out how many days pass. (Note that Shakespeare has made an error when he says that Juliet will awaken 42 hours after taking the potion—what should he have said?)

8) Find an Elizabethan tune that would be appropriate for the party scene (or write one).

9) You get the gist. Come up with a research project that interests you relating to *Romeo and Juliet* and pursue it. The more we know about a play and its elements, the better we understand and enjoy it!

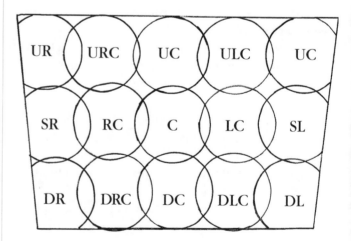

| UR | URC | UC | ULC | UC |
| SR | RC | C | LC | SL |
| DR | DRC | DC | DLC | DL |

# Bibliography

"Shakespeare and the Renaissance Concept of
    Honor"
Curtis Brown Watson
Princeton University Press 1960

"The Story of English"
McCrum Cran and MacNeil
Viking Press 1986

"Swearing and Perjury In Shakespeare's Plays"
Frances A. Shirley
George Allen and Unwin Ltd. 1979

"Dream in Shakespeare"
Marjorie B. Garber
Yale University Press 1974

"Wooing, Wedding and Power/Women In
    Shakespeare's Plays"
Irene G. Dash
Columbia University Press 1981

"Making a Match/Courtship in Shakespeare
    and his Society"
Ann Jennalie Cook
Princeton University Press 1991

"Shakespeare Lexicon and Quotation Dictionary"
Alexander Schmidt/revised Gregor Sarrazin
Dover Publications Inc. 1971

"Asimov's Guide to Shakespeare"
Isaac Asimov
Avenel Books 1978

"A New Variorum Edition of Shakespeare—Romeo
    and Juliet"
Ed. Horace Howard Furness
Dover Publications, Inc. 1963

"The Kittredge Shakespeare—Romeo and Juliet"
Ed. George Lyman Kittredge/rev. Irving Ribner
Blaisdell Publishing Co. 1966

"The Waning of the Middle Ages"
J. Huizinga
St. Martin's Press, Inc. 1949

"Shakespeare's Italy"
Ed. Marrapodi, Hoenselaars, Cappuzzo and
    Santucci
Manchester University Press 1993

"Prefaces to Shakespeare"
Harley Granville-Barker
Sidgwick and Jackson, Ltd. 1935

"The Bankside Shakespeare—Romeo and Juliet"
Ed. Appleton Morgon
The Shakespeare Society of N.Y. 1889

"The Osier Cage"
Robert O. Evans
University of Kentucky Press 1966

"Courtship in Shakespeare"
William G. Meader
King's Crown Press 1954

"New Cambridge Shakespeare—Romeo and Juliet"
Ed. G. Blakemore Evans
Cambridge University Press 1984

"Shakespeare's Philosophy of Love"
Herman Harrell Horne
Edwards and Broughton Co. 1945

"Shakespeare and Catholicism"
H. Mutschmann and K. Wentersdorf
Sheed and Ward 1952

"The Plays of Shakespeare"
Ed. Howard Staunton
G. Routledge 1858-1861

## The Set

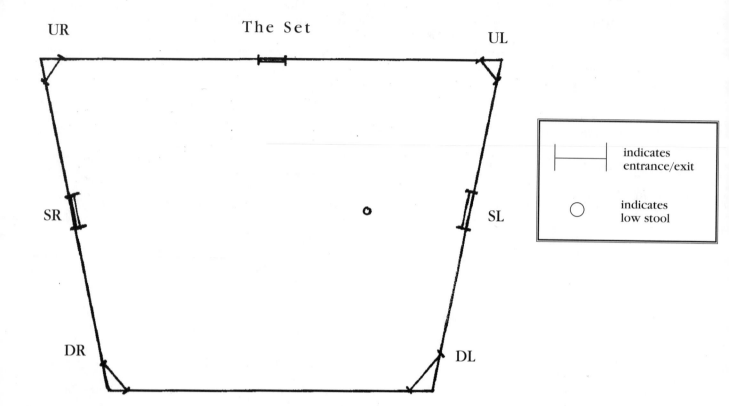